P1, 75, 111, 65, 62

WOMEN
UNDER THE
INFLUENCE

WOMEN UNDER THE INFLUENCE

Alcohol and Its Impact

Brigid McConville

Schocken Books · New York

First American edition published by Schocken Books 1985
10 9 8 7 6 5 4 3 2 1   85 86 87 88
Copyright © Brigid McConville 1983
Published by agreement with Virago Press Ltd., London

Library of Congress Cataloging in Publication Data
McConville, Brigid, 1956-
Women under the influence.
Includes bibliographical references and index.
1. Women — Alcohol use. 2. Women — Great Britain —
Alcohol use.   I. Title.
HV5137.M43   1985   362.2'92'088042   84-22237

Manufactured in the United States of America
ISBN 0–8052–3977–4 (hardbound)
0–8052–0776–7 (paperbound)

SSH

CONTENTS

Acknowledgements *vi*

Introduction *1*

PART THREE: COPING WITH DRINKING PROBLEMS

ACKNOWLEDGEMENTS

Thanks to the women of DAWN, especially Shirley Otto, Clare Wilson, Fiona Richmond and Chris Chambers who have been an invaluable source of ideas and support. Thanks also to my editor, Ruthie Petrie, who not only helped the book into shape but tried and tested its methods on her own drinking habits.

My friends and all my family have given me great encouragement, especially my sister Fran McConville, and Liz Mellon, Jane Salvage, Mark Cooper, Lou Scott, Hugh Cooper and John Shearlaw — who kept me in constant touch with my subject.

I am very grateful also to May Holland and Ronald Forbes who provided me with a great deal of information and encouragement, to Dr Roger Williams of Kings College Hospital Liver Unit who kindly had Part Two of my manuscript checked, and to Mic Cheetham, who got the whole thing off the ground in the first place.

The diagrams included here have been adapted from their originals. For permission to adapt and use, I would like to thank the Health Education Council for diagram 2, p. 78, 3, p. 82, and 4, p. 83, and Accept Services UK for diagram 5 on p. 86.

I especially want to thank all those women who gave me their time and courageously talked about their often painful experiences with alcohol. I am indebted to the women workers at AA, to the women of Women's Fightback, the Tulse Hill CR group, the Oxford House women's group and my other women friends without whom this book could not have been written.

She has thrust herself off
The shelf of the earth
Gone searching
For the white side of night.
Flight is the glass
Between her hands
Lifting her
Out of her gravity.

She climbs on the dark's back
Trusts it
Like a dolphin
To take her twisting
Along the rim
Of the world.
With every drink
She swallows a shoal of stars.

The glass is empty.
Light shatters her body
Exploding in the sea.
She hits the surface
And her mouth yawns wide,
A fish gulping air.
Nothing matters
But the wind brushing her tongue.

Liz Mellon

INTRODUCTION

Why a book about women and alcohol: surely the 'serious' drinkers are men, while we occasionally keep them company with a half of lager or a sticky cocktail? Not so: women's drinking has changed as our position as women has changed, and we are rapidly becoming major consumers of alcohol.

It has been a mixed blessing. On the one hand, we generally have more freedom to drink, more money to spend and more opportunities to enjoy drinking. But, on the other, more women are becoming ill and dying as a result of drink. This book is for *all* women drinkers, because while most of us still enjoy 'a good drink', we all have the potential to lose control of our drinking and be destroyed by it.

The recent publicity about increases in women's drinking has intensified, in some quarters, into concern about a new 'women's problem'. But we need to be wary of the focus of this concern. For example, the increase in women's drinking has been blamed on 'Women's Lib', and women's alcoholism has been called 'the ransom of emancipation'. So we need to remember how 'scare tactics' have been used against women in times of social change: the suffragettes were warned that their reproductive organs would wither, and more recently working mothers have been blamed for juvenile delinquency and mental breakdown.[1] We are now in a period when women are under huge pressure to return to the home as unemployment rises and our social services are dismantled. We need to be careful that our drinking 'problems' are put in the context of the social pressures that push us into drinking rather than in terms of a 'moral panic' about a woman's rightful place — traditionally *not* in the pub.

I became interested in writing about women's drinking when a colleague of mine told me the story of her young daughter's disability. Her child had been born with some of the symptoms of Down's syndrome, but a series of doctors were unable to agree on a diagnosis. Eventually, after years of consulting specialists, one of these suggested that her daughter might be suffering from Foetal Alcohol Syndrome, or FAS.

She had never heard of this at the time, and nor had I when she told me. I was appalled to realise that I, an enthusiastic and sometimes heavy drinker, had no clear idea of the effects of alcohol on my body. I began to find out about FAS and realised that this was only the tip of the iceberg. I didn't know and neither did my women friends, that alcohol affects us differently and more damagingly than men in all sorts of ways. Finding out about this was a struggle: there are virtually no books or articles on the subject that are well informed without being highly technical, obscure or plain inaccessible. So I set out to write a book to provide that information for women.

When I started I had no axe to grind, no theory to propound, but only my own background and family history of intermittent drinking problems. In the text books I found the occasional chapter about women drinkers, written by the experts (usually male), but from women drinkers themselves there was silence. I decided to start by interviewing as many women as possible about their own drinking, and the book starts with four of these women speaking at length about their drinking. (I have changed their names for the sake of privacy in this chapter and in subsequent ones; some place names have been changed for the same reason.)

Very soon a pattern began to emerge: very different women were saying the same sorts of things about themselves and their drinking. Whether 'social' drinkers or 'problem' drinkers, they talked about their feelings of oppression, inadequacy, shyness, anxiety, depression and lack of confidence as women.

These women come from all over the UK, and range in age from about fifteen to sixty-five; they come from different social classes and ethnic backgrounds. I interviewed them individually and in groups, through established agencies, personal contacts and women's groups.

Most of the women I talked to are white. Few Black women attend the established agencies as clients, and I came across only one Black woman worker in the alcohol field. 'We have no statistical evidence about Black women's drinking,' says Prudence Solomon of the Alcohol Counselling Service in Brixton. 'There is no education on drink, and a lot of Black women don't appreciate what can happen.' There is also likely to be a mistrust of the largely white-run services, says Jean White, also of the ACS. But from what Black women have said to me, it seems that women in the ethnic minorities have patterns of drinking — or not drinking — which are very different from those of the majority of white women.

What evidence there is, suggests that Black women are turning to drink more than previously, and that they are likely to drink at home and in secret.[2] It also seems that in Black groups, social problems tend to be contained within the community and dealt with, if at all, by the family and by the church. But if white women drink from frustration and a sense of oppression — while feeling they must hide their 'shameful' habit — how much more must Black women have reasons to do the same?

Our perceptions and patterns of drinking must be seen against a background of social attitudes and expectations. Chapter 3, which is about the stereotyped image of women drinkers as portrayed in popular literature, advertisements and the media, supplies a part of this background. These are the 'norms' against which we are measured, and if we are to make sense of our behaviour we must look critically at these social and 'moral' yardsticks. This look at the conventional ideas about women drinkers raises the question: Is there something 'wrong' with us — or with 'normality'?

The emphasis in the opening chapters is on the social factors which affect women's drinking, but the nature of our society is such that decisions by governments, advertisers and the alcohol industry have a powerful influence on our drinking habits. The last chapter of Part One looks at the statistics about drinking and the economic and political factors that shape 'normality' — and our drinking destinies.

Part Two looks at the physical effects of alcohol on our bodies. We are far more prone than men to alcohol's intoxicating and damaging effects, and we must have a series of educational campaigns to inform us of the facts — if we are to make vital choices about our own, and our children's, health.

Part Three is written for women like myself who have worried that they are drinking for reasons, and to a level, which they feel unhappy about. I have suggested ways of self-help, and professional help, for those who decide they want to cut down.

I hope that women drinkers who read this book will recognise some of their own experience, and that, at the end of it, they will be able to use alcohol more healthfully, and more happily.

PART ONE

WOMEN AND ALCOHOL

WOMEN SPEAKING

JANE

My neighbours used to say to me, 'Jane, *why* do you drink? You've got four lovely children, a good home, a good husband.' I used to blame my husband and all sorts of things, but I really didn't know why I drank. Once I started I just couldn't stop.

It was my youngest son, Malcolm, who was most affected by my drinking. He was withdrawn and didn't play with other kids. He went to a special school three days a week and he asked to be called Malcolm at one school, and Nigel, his second name, at the other.

I didn't believe it was anything to do with my drinking. I rationalised that it was his teacher's fault, or that he was like his father, a loner.

I was ashamed of myself, and full of guilt about the effect on my family and about not being a 'normal' mother. I always wanted to be a 'good' mother — one who baked and sewed and sang lullabies and kept a beautiful home. But none of those things came naturally to me.

When my babies were born I thought there was supposed to be a big wave of emotion. I didn't feel it. I thought there was something missing in me and that I was inadequate. No one told me that you just feel tired and want to sleep and forget the whole thing.

I also felt very inadequate beside my sister and sister-in-law. Men always turned and looked at my sister — she was very sexy.

My sister-in-law is a nurse, very capable. She cooked and sewed —
and she could shatter me with the lift of an eyebrow. Until about
three years ago I couldn't relate to women at all, especially women
with nursing experience.

I got all my ideas from women's magazines. No one told me it's
okay sometimes to *hate* your kids and feel trapped by children.

I came to London from Scotland when I was eighteen and I had
never had a drink. I lived with my sister and I was very unhappy.
So when I first saw the man who was to be my husband, Ken, I
said to myself — I will marry him. It was his looks. He was to be
my knight in shining armour, come to save me.

I was very immature and influenced by what others said. I
believed in happy-ever-after and thought I would be secure for the
rest of my life.

I married at nineteen and had a child in my first year. I started
taking amphetamines for depression. They made me feel good and
beautiful, and I thought then that I could match up to my sister-in-
law's standards. I remember sitting there sewing for hours.

At twenty-five I was sent to a mental hospital because of my
addiction to amphetamines. When I came out I started to go to
pubs to drink 'socially' with friends. Booze made me feel good, the
same as the pills had, and beautiful.

But I drank more than my friends. I always wanted more, drank
faster and I wanted to stay until the bell rang in the pub. I could
never stop. It still amazes me how people drink half a bottle of
wine and leave the rest. I didn't get drunk every night, just
Saturday night and Sunday lunch at that stage. It was no problem
in between at that time — only later.

But drinking crept up on me very slowly and subtly. I used to
get half a bottle of Scotch at Sunday lunch and invite a friend in. If
she had a drink with me it made it more acceptable. But I had guilt
at the back of my mind that my friends, the 'good mothers', didn't
drink.

When my eldest daughter was sixteen, the twins were eleven
and Malcolm was four, I went out to work as a telephonist. I
started drinking a lot with a younger crowd from work. I enjoyed
it. I rewarded myself. I thought I should enjoy my life now after
having had the children.

I used to stay out late. My husband took very little notice. If he
did say anything I would be angry with him. I told him he was a
moron and I needed more stimulating company. I thought I was
some kind of frustrated genius ...

He used to get up, go to work, come home and watch the telly and go to bed. He is an electrician and has been doing the same job for twenty odd years. He is a normal man, stable and happy in his way of life — but I thought something was wrong with it.

I needed to drink more and more. I started buying bottles and drinking all weekend. I couldn't cope with my family and the puberty of my daughter. She assumed the role of mother in the house and I was jealous. I was always shouting and very angry. And all through this was the guilt: I wasn't happy when I was working, and I wasn't happy when I wasn't working.

This went on for about five years, drinking whenever I could. Then one time I met an alcoholic down-and-out in a pub. I had the money, he had the time. So I went to his 'skipper' [derelict site] to drink with him.

I thought I had found Paradise — drinking cheap wine at eight o'clock on a Saturday morning. I had no responsibility. I didn't have to wash on weekends. There I was, a middle-aged woman from a comfortable home, drinking in a derelict house ... I wanted drink more than I wanted home, children or husband.

I lost my job through alcohol too. I was ready for promotion but we all got drunk in the office and later I was sacked. I started staying out later, and drinking more on weekends. I blamed my husband, blamed my children. I wanted to be free of them.

I got another job and lost it, again, through drink. I went on drinking at home then — when I could. When I had no money I had to stop. I started to lose care for myself. I became aggressive and fearful when I stopped drinking. One weekend when I was angry with my husband I swallowed a lethal dose of paracetamol — and then told him.

I used to buy a bottle with my fish and chips and drink from Thursday to Monday. My husband didn't know how to cope. He stayed out of the house, and buried himself in work, pretending it wasn't happening.

By now I had attempted suicide five times — when I was drunk and felt sorry for *me*. The last attempt ended in intensive care. I can't tell if I ever really wanted to die; I was always drunk when I did it. When I came *off* booze, in midweek, then I would have wanted to die.

After about three years of drinking at home I had no relationship with my family whatsoever. My daughter told me only last week that the children thought the lady who drank came out of a bottle; it wasn't their mum. But I didn't know this.

My children tried everything to stop me: anger, love, leaving me alone, shouting, asking why? When I said I didn't want to drink alone but I was forced to, my daughter even drank along with me. She drank as I did — but I didn't want to share my booze.

Then my eldest daughter left home, and the twins were teenagers and always staying out. Just little Malcolm was there and going to the pub for my booze. I made him come home from school to get my bottle at lunchtime. I stayed in my bedroom mostly. I was dirty. I didn't wash or cook.

I used to wander sometimes in the streets. At forty I went to the Embankment to try and be a hippy. I went to a disco that my daughter went to. I made obscene phone calls. I kept running away. My home life was just a mess. I was desperately lonely and afraid.

Then a lady I knew came to talk to me. She didn't condemn me or ask me *why* I was drinking. She just asked if I had a problem. It was a tremendous relief to be able to say yes. She spoke to me with love and understanding. She came with me to a phone box and I phoned AA [Alcoholics Anonymous]. That was six years ago.

Three beautiful women took me to a meeting in their car. I was afraid of them. I was seventeen stone and I had no decent clothes. I had to have three valium tablets and a martini to get me to my first meeting.

I was afraid of AA — I thought it was like a temperance society. But I took to it like a duck to water. I stopped drinking. I had no terrible withdrawal symptoms. I began to take an interest in myself and in my family. *It* happened. My family were thrilled. My daughter moved home again. She used to wash my hair before every meeting and call for a cab for me. Immediately the family situation got better.

It was a very slow process but I discovered I was a very *angry* woman. I was very angry at women. They petrified me. If a woman walked into the room I would always feel inferior and inadequate. Now the anger is gone.

All of my life was based on what society made me be. So many people told me to do things. Coming to *see* for myself what it really is about — that took away the anger.

Now I have an identity. I know what I like. I like being with people. I like country and western music, and I like reading. I'm not really an extrovert; I like my own company too. And I go to AA meetings two or three times a week. I've been sober now for six years.

At first I still felt guilt. I even still wanted to be a 'good mother'. I did lots of washing and cleaning — and found I was getting resentful when my daughter left the bath dirty!

But I came to realise that I was a good mother, became a sick mother and now I'm an okay mother. I'm pretty average. They love me and I love them. Yes, my identity *is* being a mother — not a wife or a career woman.

Two years ago my two sons were killed in accidents, little Malcolm six weeks after his elder brother. Without the fellowship of AA I would never have survived it.

But they both had four years of me sober before they died. Malcolm, who had been going to a special school, could by then read and write and swim and play football. My oldest was a head chef. I knew that in that time I had been a better mother to them than ever.

After a year in AA I realised that my marriage had died. We didn't want to sleep together after all those years. Now we have a good friendship. Now I am more understanding of Ken, the man. He is not in the role of protector or provider. It really is a good relationship. The children accept it. We still live together and he still works hard. He is reasonably happy. He accepts himself.

I am happy too. I have peace of mind. I believe in God. I don't know that I *love*: I like, I care, I understand. I do *care* passionately.

I don't give a damn who knows I'm an alcoholic. I couldn't say what alcoholism is. I just know I've got it, and I can do something about it. I was born with this disease and this personality, so I don't drink.

People who are not alcoholic sometimes drink for the same reasons I did — because they feel inadequate or tired. But they don't go *on* drinking. In the alcoholic, the feelings of guilt, fear and anger go *so* deep ... My anger leaves me physically and mentally exhausted even now.

I think it's okay to get angry if I'm angry for a good reason. Now I try to expend it by writing it down. It is a good thing too to redirect this anger, this fierceness. That emotion is energy. I am still angry, but not the destructive anger that turns inwards, that lasts and lasts. I don't feel that consuming guilt.

So many images are put on us whether we are male or female. It leaves you feeling that you have failed to be the Sexy Woman or the Good Mum. I don't *have* to wash and clean and sleep with my husband to be a good mother and wife. *I was* Ken's wife. I'm released from that image now.

I'm fat. People keep saying — you should slim. But I'm comfortable as I am. I'm quite happy being fourteen and a half stone. I like the image of being motherly. A fellow at our meeting said once, 'Jane, you know, you're dead sexy.' It made me want to say — ugh — go away, leave me alone.

So many women don't have a feeling of self-worth. There is so much pressure on us to be thin, to be glamorous, to be the career girl, to be happy with house and kids. Yet some of the happiest people I know are just everyday ordinary people.

If I feel down sometimes, I think — I'll put my best dress on. That will make me feel better. But it doesn't work like that. When I see people who just don't care, who are so free — they look marvellous. A lot of women don't have that freedom within.

Other people are always telling us what is going to happen — so it does happen. They told me I should be frustrated: I became so. They say women are drinking more because of the strains of being a woman today — so this is what is going to happen. The ideas come from the outside, from the media, and then they become fact. The image becomes real.

I *was* happy for a while at home when the kids were there. I liked cooking and sewing in a way — because I loved being the image that I was meant to be. I liked doing what everyone else was doing. I belonged at one stage of my life; it was lovely. But I still didn't know what *I* liked in life. When I joined AA I was forty-two and I had to look back and say, well, I enjoyed English and maths in school. So I did some 'O' levels.

For a woman to find out what she really is, to be proud of it, to believe in it and accept it is the most important thing: just to *be*.

JULIE

I remember distinctly the first time I got drunk. I was on a pre-university course in France. I was eighteen. We were sitting in a café, about twenty of us, all students. I got a bit pissed — and then just wanted to see how much I could drink.

I puked up in bed that night, in my sleep, and woke up with vomit all over my bedclothes. It was really quite dangerous. But I wasn't appalled by it. I felt it was quite an achievement being able to go over the top. That occasion was my first social encounter with the opposite sex. I was quite nervous and I also wanted to be 'one of the boys'.

Everyone else was going to university after the course except me. I was going to do nursing and I felt a bit embarrassed about it and inadequate. So I didn't tell them at first. My brother — who had been on the course before — made me feel that nursing was for people who were a bit stupid. I didn't really want to be a nurse, but it was that or secretarial — or being a wife.

I had been to a school where we weren't encouraged to do 'A' levels. If you went into the sixth form you did French and driving lessons. I have felt intellectually inadequate from the time I was in school. I was always at the bottom of the class. Except once, when I came third. I felt really guilty about it as I thought everyone else must have thought I was cheating.

I used to drink during that time in France in the same way that I do now — because I have to depend on my personality to make a statement rather than on my achievements.

I also used drinking to stop me from developing the female side. I could become 'one of the boys', and by drinking with men we could be more like brothers and avoid any sexual tensions.

I became part of a group on the course that was more interested in drinking than in going to museums — and we had a whale of a time. I was the jolly, hearty one. Most of the others were boys and I kept up with them socially when it was over.

I was friends with some of the girls too. They were clever. I went to see one of them in Cambridge afterwards when I was nursing and she said to me, 'Are you still washing nappies then?' I felt I was doing a dummy job. It's one of the reasons I eventually left nursing.

I started the nursing course when I got back to London, and drank quite a lot then. It has been part of my reputation ever since. I got in with Australian agency nurses who drank Fosters and we had beer breakfasts. We used to meet at a pub in Piccadilly after a really exhausting night on duty and get pissed.

It was good fun, a good opportunity to act ridiculous. The other Australian nurses were very funny and lively and open. We had a 'what the hell, nothing matters' attitude. It was pleasure-seeking. Many of the other nurses came from very different working-class backgrounds. They drank 'ladylike' drinks in the pub. I didn't feel very comfortable with them.

I had no really close friends at that time. I don't think I knew what that meant. I was ploughing around, always searching for something, without a clue what for. I had no place to settle down or relax.

I also hated nursing. I was very nervous and unsatisfied in the job. Drinking was a way of forgetting about it completely and relaxing. If I had time off I *had* to go out and enjoy myself. I was bored by myself. I needed distracting entertainment.

My nursing training course lasted from when I was nineteen to when I was twenty-three. I lived in a flat with a friend for some of that time. We had a lot of dinner parties and without fail I knew I would be sick from drinking at the end of every evening. It was only wine and we couldn't afford great quantities, but my tolerance wasn't as high then as it is now. I can't be sick now. I drank then because I was nervous and I was trying to appear more capable and social than I was.

After I finished my training I left nursing completely. I drank a fantastic amount then and went to a lot of parties. It was the first time I became quite alarmed at how much I was drinking.

I had met up with an old friend, Jenny, and I was very attracted to her. I wasn't surprised in myself. I knew something was always there. But I had no clue what to do about it — and I felt absolutely disgusted with myself. I was obsessive about her and I had absolutely no one I could tell. I wouldn't dare. So I used to write reams of poetry — or what I called poetry. And I was getting drunk all the time.

Drink is definitely a tool for me. I use it to get things *out*. The more pissed I get the less inhibited I am and I can express emotions that wouldn't be accepted normally. And people say, 'Oh, she's just pissed' — so it's not taken too seriously.

I use it to get over the first step to expressing things I have kept inside of myself, some of them quite positive things. Drink can help make those feelings towards people into a reality. Then it's established, I'm over a hurdle — and the next day I can deal with that reality.

With Jenny I was always testing her out, seeing how far I could go in expressing my feelings without her actually *knowing*. It was totally naive. She didn't understand what was going on. How we managed to maintain our friendship I don't know.

I put on about a stone in weight at the time. I had always been a seven stone weakling and when I went over eight stone it was the first time I recognised my body. I got more bottom and boobs. It alarmed me — I had always been slightly anorexic. I didn't want to be feminine; the boy in me was strong.

When I was little I was in the Anti-Dust Society. My older brother said all women were dust, and if I wanted to play with him (and there was no one else around) I had to be part of the Anti-Dust Society. So I had to dislike all females and anything feminine. I played with tanks and airplanes, not dollies. I had a little boy identity.

At the same time a friend of mine was pressurising me to go travelling with her, and apart from not wanting to leave, I was frightened of travelling in the 'big world'. I really didn't want to go, so I drank my way through until the day we left.

Other people were worried about how much I was drinking, especially my mother. A friend of hers had told her that I would be an alcoholic by the time I was forty if I wasn't careful. I didn't believe it. I knew *why* I was drinking, so I wasn't afraid of becoming an alcoholic, and I could go without drink for some days.

I did eventually go travelling with my friend but I was utterly miserable. I got terribly bad spots which took a year to go away. All the time I was travelling I was sorting out the idea — was I lesbian? I had already made a decision, in fact — which was that I would always be pursuing this question mark about my sexuality. That was why I was drinking.

When I came back, I lived in my parents' flat in London. Whenever they went out, or went away for the weekend, I would hit the gin bottle. It was lovely. I was always drinking *his*, my father's drink. I was getting something back on him.

I was also very careful and scared about replacing it. One time I took two bottles of wine that turned out to be terribly expensive and rare. I looked everywhere for replacements and eventually found some at Justerini and Brooks. They told me the bottles were too young to drink. So when my father took them out for a dinner party I was longing to say to him, 'Don't you think they're a bit young?'

Then for a while I had a job working with mentally handicapped kids. Jenny was living nearby and we met up with a crowd who drank fantastic amounts and spent loads of money. Jenny and I decided to share a flat together and I started being able to articulate my feelings for her.

I talked to her generally about my anxieties that I was attracted to women, and she accepted that it was a part of me. We used to sleep in the same bed, like sisters, holding hands. But I couldn't bear it in the end. I felt very angry with her too. I was drinking a lot to get through those conversations with her. I did make my attraction for her explicit somehow. I told her in a pizza palace that I *really, really* loved her. She understood it but didn't feel the same way. So I had to deal with it and withdraw a lot of the things I had put on to her. She stayed incredibly loyal and supportive.

Then I got so depressed that I couldn't work. I kept getting panics at work, feeling really claustrophobic. I wanted to lash out, to explode. Instead I would sweat and feel very hot. I spent three days in bed smoking myself stupid, on a destructive trip. And then I decided I would have to do something about it.

I started doing psychotherapy. It relieved a lot of tension. It didn't alter the problem, but it made me more able to cope with it. I felt that I wasn't so bad, that I should look after myself more instead of trying to destroy myself.

I moved to a flat in Clapham where I felt very safe and settled. I loved being there and the security took away the need to drink. I went on a vegetarian binge. I was very healthy, but a bit neurotic in a different way — about food. For a year I hardly had a drink.

Then I took a job working with maladjusted boys, which was depressing. They used to pinpoint my vulnerability, asking me about my sex life. At the same time I started a new course of pottery at art school. It was a first glimmer for me; I knew I had a feeling for it and I wanted to do more.

And I was having my first sexual experience with a woman, Jean, at about this time. It was not satisfactory. She didn't want to talk about it and it left me feeling that I still had to go on resolving something. I knew I'd have to have another affair with a woman to sort it out. I wanted to get out of London and out of the relationship.

That was part of the reason why I moved down to Devon to work as an apprentice potter. I had a fairly abstemious time there until I met George. He had come down for the weekend to stay with a friend, and we got arseholed drunk, from Friday night to Sunday. And on Sunday I slept with him.

Drink made it much easier. I felt, if I get pissed I can do this. And we did have good sex for the first part of our relationship. But we always had to be pissed. We never did it sober or in the afternoon. It was always in the dark when we came back from the pub.

We saw each other on weekends for about four or five months, and as I had never felt near to being relaxed with a man I thought — this must be *it*. He had been asking me to get married for ages, jokingly, but I didn't take it as a joke.

I thought — well, why not? I'm getting married. It was partly that I wanted to give a reassurance to my parents that I was okay. I have always seen marriage as part of my future. I can't see myself as being alone when I'm older and marriage seems the only way not to be.

I thought we could live in the village, have children and I'd run a pottery. I haven't exorcised that little fantasy yet. We even set the date and he was going to tell my parents.

But there was something about my feelings for women that was not resolved and I felt I wanted to see Jean again. I started withdrawing from my relationship with George. We had a terrible row, white anger, and we used to physically fight. I felt suddenly very trapped and wanted to get out. I feel now that I was very unfair to him.

Sex was spoiled. I didn't want him to touch me. When we did have sex I would have to be blotto. I was drinking a lot. I felt he didn't know *me*, he just wanted to have sex with me. It was only partly true, but I focused on it.

I went to see Jean — and slept with her. I felt then that I couldn't carry on with George. All those feelings in me towards women were really much stronger.

The golden opportunity to get out came when a friend in London offered me a place in the house where I live now. That's when I started my ceramics course, and I started going to the Women's Therapy Centre.

I am much more determined now to sort things out. Drinking gives me the energy to face things with women. I feel I have to be hard on myself and steam through things that I had thought a lot about. Drink helps me to do something about it and to talk with my friends.

We have lots of boozy dinner parties in the house. I find I try to get close to people in an aggressive way when I'm drinking. I provoke people to get close to them and establish a relationship.

I always suffer from terrible anxiety and remorse in the morning. I feel terribly guilty about the way I've behaved because I know women aren't supposed to get drunk like that — and angry that it's *because* I'm a woman that I feel so bad.

Usually if I wake up in a really jerky frame of mind it's because I've been talking very personally to someone, usually about sexuality, and gone too far.

There was a time when I had to ring people at four or five in the morning to ask if I had told them something about myself. Especially Jenny — I used to worry that I had told her that I fancied her. I can never remember exactly what happened the night before.

I'm worried that people won't like me any more after I've been drinking, yet I use all the tools — being aggressive and demanding — to make people reject me. I keep doing that. I feel frightened about it. That's what worries me about drink — not that I'll be sitting in a bar till closing time forever — but simply my potential to be hurtful.

I'm in a new relationship with a woman now, Sue — and we always have a few drinks on Friday evenings. It's a real way of relaxing. But then I go beyond the relaxing stage. I take the lid off my censorship and all these worms that are wriggling around, start flicking out ...

Last Friday I had an awful row with Sue. I had felt some anger with her, but not to the extent that I expressed. It seems I'm angry with people for my own reasons and not because of anything they've done to me.

But I do feel real anger about having an affair with a woman. She dominates me by *giving*, and sorting things out for me. She forces me to get on with things that I would otherwise put off. I feel afraid of being taken over. I feel like a child.

After nights like last Friday I wake up early with lots of energy. I have to get up and start doing things. I get jerky, things keep popping up in my head. I keep remembering them and feeling shocked. I feel absolutely, utterly ... uuuugh ... I can't stand it really ... really sensing something about me that I don't want to exist. I want to forget it, not face up to the idea that it exists.

The next morning I always say — that's it. *No* more. I must control myself now. I don't trust myself any more not to attack people.

I know that through drink I am testing how much people can take, how much they love you. I push to the limit. In making Sue angry last weekend I found a new level with her. I found limits in our relationship which I have been seeking. In relationships between women you have to shape your own boundaries more than in relationships between men and women, which have rules and limits set from the start.

I enjoy drinking too. You create what feels like devastation and force people to get on to that level with you. It forms a bond that you might not achieve otherwise — which *is* creative. People have never actually gone from me as a result. You feel much closer to people after that incredible writhing around.

MIRIAM

I have always been attracted to drink. I liked it when the grown-ups drank. They all seemed so much more cheerful — except that my mother looked silly when she got tiddly. After seeing how she behaved, I always forced myself not to show the effects of drink.

Whenever we went out, drinking seemed the thing to do. I wanted to be 'one of the boys' and I used to drink more than the other women. I desperately wanted a boyfriend. I was terribly afraid of people and drink took away my inhibitions. I thought if I got a fella I would be okay — and I did, I had lots of them.

Women frightened me. I was so insecure in my own femininity. I didn't seem to belong anywhere as a woman. I never felt part of anything, and it seemed like everyone else did.

I had a reputation for being a good drinker. People used to call me 'hollow legs'. But I often felt the ill-effects without letting it show. I used to go off and be sick and come back and continue drinking. And I didn't like non-drinking company. I always wanted other people to have one too.

I was married straight from school, because I was pregnant, and I had two children before I was twenty. I had never had a job. I could go weeks without a drink at that time — I was too busy with the children.

Men were more chauvinistic in those days. We had always done what my husband said. He was in the Forces and so we moved a lot. I enjoyed that. I always felt the next place might be the place I belonged to; it might be what I was looking for.

We never lived anywhere longer than two years, by which time I was always raring to go. I took on a new image each time. I would be the Arty one, or the Hippy one. And as soon as we got established, I wanted to go. I couldn't keep the front up permanently.

It was the same with jobs. They were all just images, not *me*. I had so many images, so many faces, that I lost track of my personality. I had no idea who I was. I once met some people from the drinking scene when I was on my way back from work and they didn't recognise me.

I was aware of how I felt at the time. I had worried about who was the real me from the time I was fourteen. I drank to drown all that.

Then in my late twenties, my marriage broke up. I felt a great sense of freedom. It was the first real decision I had ever made. At last, I had no grown-up appendage. I was on my own and the freedom to drink was one of the many freedoms I had — like smoking in bed. I liked the image, and there was no one to frown and say, 'That's not done.'

I had sexual freedoms too and as many boyfriends as I wanted. But they were baggage for the journey and I felt terribly guilty. I also felt a lot of guilt about my children. Right from the start I felt as inadequate as a mother as I did as a woman. They were both Doctor Spock babies, and I was mostly concerned about the image they created. They had to *look* right. I was always busy organising them, but it didn't come from the inside.

17

Drink anaesthetised those feelings. I was like an ostrich, I thought if I put my head in the sand no one would see me. But I used to wake up and worry at three o'clock in the morning.

The children were about seven and nine at the time. They used to think I was occasionally ill, but they say now that they never connected it with drink.

Then I met someone who moved in with us and I started drinking regularly and heavily. I had my first blackout at that time. When I 'came to' I had cooked and served a meal and was getting ready for my son's birthday party. Everything was neat and tidy — and I couldn't remember anything that had happened.

No one else had noticed anything odd about me. I asked my kids, 'Did we have a nice lunch? Who washed up? Who served?' It terrified me and I buried it immediately. Later I turned it into a joke. I said to my boyfriend, 'That was a nice drink you gave me the other day.' The only way I could handle it was to tell it as a funny story.

Then I met the man who was to be my second husband. I liked him because he drank such a lot and was always happy to open a bottle at any time. We seemed a perfect match. But very soon after he moved in it wasn't so good. We quarrelled and he used to beat me. I blamed it on myself. I thought it was to do with my drinking and how I carried on with other men. I always took the blame, and after a while it would always get better. I was terrified of him going and was continually persuading him to stay.

I thought I was really in love. I needed him to direct my life. I believed I didn't know how to cope or what to do without him. But I always *had coped* with bills and so on. Yet once I got someone with a stronger personality, I felt I just couldn't. He organised everything.

Even on our first date when we went out to dinner I said, 'Oh, you order for me, I'm fed up with making decisions. I've got too many of them to make.' It was wonderful to give all the responsibility to someone else. I had always had the feeling that everyone else was right and I was wrong.

Then he wanted to move to another flat, because of his job. The children were very upset but I ignored their wishes. He said we *will* move; he had all the arguments — and so we moved.

I was away from all my friends as a result and we were always with his friends. I trotted along behind him, doing everything that he did. We drank a lot and sexually we were 'swinging'. We went to a lot of partner-swapping parties. It all added to my sense of separateness from everyone else. At work I was very prim and proper while my private life was really very odd.

This went on for about five years. I would drink a lot, then take time off work and drink at home. By the time I went to the pub to meet people I was already drunk. The drinking at home didn't count because it wasn't measured. I had no idea how much I drank, although I could have a bottle and a half of spirits without noticing. Then I'd be surprised when I felt drunk after having one drink at the pub.

He was beating me a lot at that time. I had to explain away black eyes and broken bones — but I loved the secrecy of our sex lives. I never blamed him. I hated him sometimes, but I was totally dependent on him. He was my reason for being.

Then he left me, and I was horrified to find out that I hadn't even noticed he had gone until one or two days had passed. The kids had to tell me that he had gone. I was so shocked about not noticing it that I began to think that perhaps drink *was* a problem. Until then I had convinced myself that drink was a good thing; if there was a problem, it was me, not drink.

I decided to go to an AA meeting. It was a great relief to discover there that I wasn't any different to anyone else. Things like wetting the bed that I had been so ashamed of — I used to blame him — I realised that it happened to other people too.

It was agonising physically but I did stop drinking. I felt so wonderful that I thought — I *can* manage without him. As soon as I said that, he came back.

Life picked up again as it was before, and for the first time I realised just how heavily he was drinking. I felt very superior to him — and to the other AA members. So I stopped going to meetings.

I didn't drink alcohol for quite a few months. I had orange juice when we went to the pub. But one time, when it got towards closing time, I felt so bored that I thought I would have *one* drink. It gave me a real lift. I remembered that first warm feeling as it goes down. I thought — I've cracked it, I'm fortunate, I can control it.

I did for a while. But by Christmas I was out of control again. His response was to say we had better stop going to all those parties. But I didn't want to stop. I thought it was the good bit of our relationship.

At weekends there would be loads of housework to do. I would open the fridge in the morning to take the milk out, but I would always take a few swigs from a bottle of wine as well. Everything would go fuzzy at the edges. I couldn't do anything then, but I still drank.

Eventually he said, 'We'll get married.' I went along with it. If he had said, 'We'll stand on our heads in the corner,' I would have done it. I had no will-power left.

We got married on Friday the thirteenth, the weekend of the Queen's Jubilee holiday. We spent the weekend drinking, but I couldn't get drunk. I didn't get back to work the next week. I went to bed with someone else when he wasn't there. I thought — that's it. Now I've cocked the whole thing up altogether.

I had thought with the marriage that it would all be okay and there I was, I'd done it again. I told him about it and he didn't mind. He suggested I go back to the AA and I said okay. I started going to meetings and stopped drinking again. I was very angry about it this time. I didn't like them at AA. They seemed so straight-laced, po-faced and boring. My life seemed to be stretching out into one long boring tunnel of sobriety.

Everyone at AA was very 'nice', their husbands all went to Al-Anon, they had 'nice' kids. Whereas I had to sneak off after meetings to meet him in the pub. I was embarrassed too when he used to come and get me and everyone could see he was drunk. I didn't know how to adjust my feelings towards him. I thought I had depended on him so much, yet we just couldn't seem to cooperate together.

I used to have a mouthful of his beer now and then, but by Christmas I had more or less accepted that I couldn't drink at all.

We tried to carry on the same life as before but it didn't work. I had to leave him. He cracked up. It was as if we had swapped roles — he was begging *me* not to leave *him*.

I was in my early thirties then. I have more acceptance of life as it is now than I used to. I have found that you can go on being one of the angry ones in AA. Different AA groups have different characters and we are lucky in London to have so many different groups.

I have seen various patterns of women's drinking. Some drink at home alone because it makes them feel a bit naughty, a bit independent. The younger ones who are in professional jobs drink because it's *there*. They especially are under a lot of pressure.

And lots of women — and men — suffer from the identity thing like I did. You feel as if you are separated from everyone by a big glass wall. It feels as if everyone else has the rule book and you haven't.

I never knew what was 'right' and so it seemed easier to do what was 'bad'. At least I knew what the effect would be when I did the bad thing. I never knew why you should be a good girl.

I felt I had all these inadequacies in me and I chose alcohol to cover them up. I identify very much with my mother, but she gets over her problems with sheer grit and determination. Maybe I couldn't do that as a result of her being so strong.

I think anyone can be a latent alcoholic. It's to do with something spiritual. Anybody successful throughout civilisation has always had a spiritual life, values connected to religion, which we no longer have.

That lack of values, lack of self-worth can be disguised by building a huge ego around it. I knew what a shy, frightened person I was but if I told any of my friends they wouldn't have believed me.

ELLY

You wouldn't have thought I was a boozer when I was younger. I was a dancer, a member of the Royal Academy. One summer season when I was twenty-three I met the man who was to be my husband. Oh, I believed marriage was totally romantic. I had seen too many Hollywood movies. I thought he would be my slave for ever more, give me freedom, financial security ... Love? I didn't know the meaning of the word.

My first baby came after I had been married a year, and then my second one. I wasn't unhappy. I loved my babies. We were reasonably well off, we had babysitters, help in the house.

But I wanted to keep up my work and I was offered the chance to do some choreography. But we lived near my mother-in-law and she was horrified at the idea. I felt really guilty that I had such wicked thoughts — a married woman with babies. Good Lord, that should be enough! They made me feel I shouldn't have got married if I wanted to work. I should have told them to take a running jump and done the job.

I didn't really want to have a third baby and I developed a terrible hang-up about sex. Intellectually I knew that sex should be enjoyed, but I was afraid of getting pregnant again. I went to a doctor and she gave me tranquillisers — the heavy barbiturate type — for my 'bad nerves' as she put it. She sent me to a psychiatrist too.

I didn't think I was barmy, I thought I was very *interesting* really. I considered myself an 'artiste' with an 'e', not a suburban housewife. I thought of myself as a martyr, you see.

But I did get pregnant and have a third baby. After that I got very thin, really scraggy. The District Nurse suggested to my husband that he give me a quick tonic of egg and sherry whipped up together every morning. He used to mix it for me — I liked being looked after — and it made me feel, well, I don't know — it's not so bad being a suburban housewife after all ...

Eventually I started mixing my own, and because I thought I was putting on too much weight I decided to cut out the egg. My husband came home unexpectedly one lunchtime. He looked at me and laughed and said, 'You're pissed.' We thought it was a huge joke. We never realised the danger.

The sherry was the beginning of my drinking, but I didn't feel it was a problem. I was still taking tranquillisers and alcohol. They played havoc with my emotions. I got very high and then very depressed.

I went back to my psychiatrist and he mumbled something about not drinking alone before sundown, and gave me more pills, purple hearts. Everyone in those days was given them. They made you feel marvellous, intellectual, bright, glamorous. He gave me two a day. I went back and asked for three. I explained I had one in the morning when I sent the kids off to school, one when they came back for lunch, and I wanted one more for the evening and putting them to bed. I still didn't think I was addicted to pills — or booze — it didn't apply to me.

He gave me the extra pills. They meant a great deal to me. I remember sitting down one day and counting them out. Enoch Powell was Minister for Health at the time, and he made a speech about the nation's huge drug bill and I remember feeling very guilty about it.

I was in one big neurotic mess. I couldn't cope and I couldn't admit it. I had terrible depressions when I came down from the booze and pills. So I was put in a mental hospital and given ECT. That was dreadful, like kicking a wireless to make it go.

But I did like the other patients. There were a lot of other women there who had trouble coping with their families. I liked being institutionalised. All my daily chores were done for me, washing and cooking and cleaning. I still wanted to be a little girl really. My mother-in-law looked after the kids. I think she loved taking my place — I should have realised what was going on.

It was when I came out of hospital that my marriage started to go wrong. We went on holiday with some friends to Austria. We all drank quite a lot then. My husband fell in love with an Austrian girl. I went berserk. They didn't have an affair or anything at the time, but I *knew* he was in love with her. I felt terribly jealous and insecure. I could have killed her — and him.

Let's face it, I was no fun at that time. I was full of pills and booze, I nagged him, I was selfish, wanting my own way all the time. But when he realised he had found my weak spot he started to torment me with this girl — and he was relentless.

I wasn't worried about losing *him*. I was worried about the financial situation. What would I do with the children and no money? It sent me bananas. He told me that he had promised to go back after the holiday and meet her. But when we got back to England he denied it all.

I think he found the responsibility of family life too difficult really. He was totally dependent on his mother who lived very near. She held the purse strings. We were all dependent on her. She had a hotel where we went to eat every Sunday and sometimes the meals were even sent round to us.

I wanted him to be a husband and a father. But he realised that there was no way we could live without his mother. He knew how much emotional pain I was in, but he kept putting the knife in and turning it at every opportunity. I became mentally sick about it. He would leave letters from the Austrian girl lying about and then deny it all. He was terribly cruel.

We had definitely fallen out of love at this stage. I don't think I ever did really love him. If I had we might have been able to cope. During this time he persuaded me that I needed to go to London — we lived in Broadstairs — for a rest. At first I didn't want to go. I knew something terrible was about to happen, but the truth was so painful that I could only glance at bits of it at one time. I wasn't drinking much at the time, just taking the pills.

I went to London and stayed with my family. I kept trying to ring him in Broadstairs but there was no reply. I used to do it from a phone box so my parents wouldn't suspect that anything was wrong.

Then one day my sister came around with a letter for me from Leo, my husband. It was a very clever letter. It said something like, 'As you've always wanted, you can stay where you are in London with Laura' — our youngest daughter. His mother was meant to take the other two girls. There was nothing in the letter about how I was to see them, or the house.

It felt like an electric shock going through me. I was in a terrible state. My family said I had to go back to Broadstairs at once and they came with me. When we got there all the locks had been changed, so I climbed up some scaffolding and through a window and let my father in through the front door. Leo was there all the time. He was in the process of making the house into three flats.

Well, I got a solicitor. I had to get the children back. There were weeks to wait. But I still had this incredible sense of loyalty to Leo! I still thought that something would happen, that everything would be okay.

In court he said I was mentally unstable. I was asked stupid things like — did I let the children play in the road? I said — of course, right in the middle. It was so stupid. Luckily my psychiatrist came to court and said I was okay and capable of looking after my children. I was even beginning to doubt my own sanity by then.

I got a legal separation with maintenance — five pounds for me and five shillings for each of the children. It was 1961 and the divorce laws weren't so good.

There was no drink on the scene at this stage, only sleeping pills. I was frightened, alone in that house with three small children. I didn't even know how to mend a fuse. I bought hundreds of candles and stuck them in every drawer of the house in case. Ridiculous.

Then I became unwell. I thought it was exhaustion, but by the spring I was really very ill. My doctor said, 'Pull yourself together, no wonder you're losing your husband' — that sort of thing. Really, I could crucify her now.

I had TB in fact and had to go to a sanatorium for three months. While I was away Leo didn't pay my maintenance and I had to go to court again. I realised he and his family wanted me to fail so that they could have the children. It was frightening to know that. Next thing was a letter from the Building Society to say he hadn't paid the mortgage and I had to leave. He had deliberately dispossessed me of the house.

It was a dreadful trauma. We had to come up to London and live in a terraced house with no bathroom and an outdoor toilet. It was a big come down for me. My income was then £12.50 a week. I paid six pounds in rent. I don't know how we managed.

I wasn't meant to work for a year because of the TB, but a woman came from the DHSS and said it was time I got a job. I was furious, I thought I had enough on my plate. But I did get a job, office work at a reasonable salary. We got by. I wasn't drinking. I was still on the purple hearts. I knew I had to make a desperate attempt to bring up my children. I also knew that deep down I wasn't equipped to do it. But with the help of pills I would.

Then one year my union, NALGO, had a cheap drink offer for

Christmas. I thought it was a marvellous idea. The previous Christmas had been so painful. It was very shameful being a single mother. I felt the stigma of being separated.

The drink came in November, but by Christmas I had drunk the lot. At no time was I drunk, but it was like putting petrol in a car. It got me started. That was the beginning of compulsive drinking for me. I started to become irresponsible, not paying the bills. I was drinking a quarter of a bottle of gin each evening, regularly. When I went home the kids would offer me tea, but I said no, I'll have a drink. It relieved the tension. I could listen to their problems then and it made me feel better.

But money was very limited and I started not to care about budgeting. One week I rationalised that if I got a big bottle, I wouldn't have to go out again. It all went very quickly.

Then we got evicted. It was terrible. I was terrified. I gave up my job as I didn't want them to know about my drinking in the office. I realised that my behaviour was noticeable. I was edgy and unreliable and continuously late in the mornings. When I felt unwell myself I didn't dare take time off because I needed it for when the children were ill. I had to pill myself up to get to work. I was desperate. So I decided to work as a temp as I would have only myself to answer to. I was kidding myself of course: I knew that when I gave up my regular job I could cash in my pension fund contributions and the money would get me out of a hole — and I could drink more.

At this time Leo, my husband, came to see me and told me that if I took him back to court — to get my home back — he would stop payments to me altogether.

I moved to a half-way house with the kids then. I used to suffer terrible depressions. I rang the Samaritans once and said I was going to kill myself with pills and booze and gave them my children's address. They asked me if I had a drink problem, and I said no, my problem was I didn't have enough money to buy drink. They put me in touch with some AA members who came and took me to a meeting.

I thought that they were lovely people, and if *I* was an alcoholic I would definitely join … I kept going to meetings but I was still drinking very heavily. I heard them talking about alcoholism as an illness and I thought, no, I'm not an alcoholic. *I'm* drinking because I've got problems.

I was so full of guilt that I was saying it was my fault. I felt I was worthless. I had no self-esteem — but plenty of arrogance.

My kids decided behind my back that they were going to live

with my mother-in-law. It was such a blow. I made a serious suicide attempt and ended up in Ealing Alcoholics Unit. I was in for three months. I kept writing to the children but I never heard from them. I used to think, I can get sober if the children come back. But then I realised I couldn't put conditions on my sobriety. I had to learn sufficient self-esteem on my own account.

I stopped drinking. I had to learn to live in the real world without props. If I was rich I would have gone on drinking indefinitely. If I'd married the sort of man I wanted — one who hid the facts of life from me — I'd be dead today.

Through AA meetings I built up my self-respect. I found the spiritual tone off-putting at first, until I learned not to confuse spirituality with religion.

Alcoholism comes in people, not in bottles. It means that the thought of going without alcohol is unimaginable — even when a doctor gives you pills and tells you not to drink you can't stop. Both of my grandfathers were alcoholics.

My kids drink. It doesn't follow that they're likely to be alcoholics. They've seen what happened to me. They did come back to me very gingerly and one at a time. We have a very good open relationship now. They know alcoholism is an illness, they know I was emotionally immature. I'm not terribly worried about their drinking.

They used to test me by pooling their pocket money to buy a bottle of wine to drink with their beans on toast. After supper they used to mark the bottle and put it in the refrigerator to see if I would drink any. It made me furious at first. I told them about it at my AA meetings and they laughed and reminded me it would take time for my kids to recover too.

I did take my husband to court again two years ago. I wanted a lump sum to compensate for the frittering away of my assets. I'm fifty-six now and I've got no savings because I kept a roof over those kids' heads for all those years.

He's remarried now and he's very wealthy. He moved to Alderney when I took him to court and all his money was tied up there — so he got away with it. He has sent me a bounced cheque since that's not enforceable.

I think now he's an absolute shit, to be perfectly honest. It's astonishing to think that our marriage lasted nearly ten years. When I saw him in court the last time, I was free of fear because I've got rid of a lot of hang-ups. But he was all sweaty and anxious. I looked at him and felt nothing but intense hatred. Now I've got three lovely daughters, and grandchildren. I've got their love and respect and my own self-respect.

I don't feel any more that I am deprived or inadequate because I don't have a husband. I don't have to be a sex-pot. I can be *me*. It's wonderful to have come out the other side. We haven't half been brain-washed, us women.

I don't think I am a feminist. There are still a lot of conflicts about women's roles. I didn't really want to go out to work. I was happy with the kids. They used to say, 'We love it when you're home, Mum.' And I don't think a lot of men want to go out to work any more than I did.

I do like men, but I know the man I married was a toad. They say you've got to kiss a lot of toads before you meet a handsome prince, but I don't think I will meet one now. I feel quite comfortable with myself. There is no search any more.

But I do think, listening to women at AA meetings, that their drinking has a lot to do with women's expected role in marriage — and the questioning of those values. Things are getting better but we've still got a long way to go. I have read feminist literature and recognised things in it. I've said, 'Yes, *I* know that.' Yes, I suppose I am a bit of a feminist ...

WHY DRINKING IS A FEMINIST ISSUE

In this chapter four women talk about the place that alcohol holds in their lives. The details of their lives are very different. The women were born years apart, in different parts of Britain, into differing social classes and expectations. Their experience of jobs, marriage, money and family are as varied as their personalities.

I approached each of them with a list of questions and each time the list was abandoned as the women started to talk — and answered my questions along the way. To them, it seemed impossible to separate their drinking habits from the context of their whole lives, which is why each interview is like a short life story. These women have described their drinking experiences not in terms of when, where, and how much, but in terms of how they feel about themselves, their families, work, relation-ships and sexuality. And individual as these women are, the same themes emerge from their different accounts.

Each one connects her drinking to the feeling that there is something 'wrong' with herself as a woman, a woman who is unable to fit comfort-ably into the expected role of wife/mother/worker/lover.

Each one feels guilt that she is not doing what she 'should' be doing, being what she 'should' be, as a woman.

Each woman suffers from a sense of personal inadequacy and low self-esteem which, after the temporary relief of drinking, is lower still.

Drink has offered an avenue of escape from these feelings, and an escape from boredom or frustration with home, work or relationships. Alcohol is also the tool used by these women to fight the inhibitions and restrictions that hedge them about. In Julie's case it has sometimes proved useful, but for the others, it eventually proved destructive.

Each account conveys the same sense of having been through something and emerged on the other side of it after a struggle. Each woman has thought long and deeply about her experience and in consequence her life has changed radically.

But should we believe what these women say? The alcohol professionals are traditionally sceptical of what drinkers say about themselves as self-delusion and deviousness are said to be part and parcel of problem-drinking.

It is true that these women have been influenced in the way they articulate and rationalise their experience — most evidently by AA and by psychotherapy. There is a certain repressive strain in AA practice, and the women who have been through the AA programme tend to denigrate their desires and aspirations as unhealthy egotism. Elly, for instance, pokes fun at her own wish to be 'an "artiste" with an "e"'.

Yet these women *have emerged*, sometimes from the prospect of total disaster, and so the terms in which they express their experiences do naturally reflect something of the means of their 'salvation'. I believe these accounts ring true — true to themselves and true to the experiences of many other women I have talked to about drinking — and that women reading them will recognise this.

Each of these women has felt that her drinking was a 'problem', of a more or less serious nature. What, then, have their experiences to do with other women, 'social drinkers' whose drinking has been less troublesome?

The answer is, a great deal. There were times in the lives of all four when alcohol was not a problem. And yet problems did develop for a variety of reasons — psychological, economic, physiological, social — out of these apparently problem-free times. What happened to each of them could, and will, happen to many other women.

There are no definitive differences between 'social drinkers' and potential 'alcoholics'. Many workers and academics in the alcohol field now agree that the experience of drinking is a continuum: we all stand somewhere on it, and differences between us are largely a matter of degree.

I hope that women who read the accounts of Julie, Jane, Miriam and Elly will identify with at least some of the things they say. I believe they are talking about the same feelings which preoccupy most women, drinkers or not, and that these feelings have their roots in our inferior economic and social position.

These are personal stories, yet they have a political significance. Each 'emergence', although very different in detail, follows the same path. Julie, Jane, Miriam and Elly began their drinking careers in isolation. Each felt that her 'problem' — whether to do with sexuality, home, work or marriage — was exclusively her own and in some way her own fault.

The guilt, anxiety and shame that each one felt, to be intensified in the vicious circle of dependent drinking, was in part a consequence of this sense of individual responsibility for 'failure'.

In time, they each came to see their 'failure' in terms of imposed social expectations about what women are supposed to be. Having once felt 'wrong' for being 'unable' to measure up to the stereotypical image of womanhood, they began to question whether there isn't something 'wrong' with that image. In the process, they each emerged from isolation, ceased to accept total blame for their drinking and came to see it in a wider context. Women's drinking can only be understood in this wider social and political context.

SOCIAL DRINKING

So far, the focus has been on women who have felt that, at some stage of their lives, drinking has been a 'problem'. But what of the majority of women who have never been labelled 'problem drinker' or 'alcoholic'?

The women speaking in this chapter see themselves as 'social' drinkers, but this does not mean that their drinking is just a simple social pleasure. Lack of confidence, low self-esteem, boredom, frustration, relief from stress: these reasons have been given for 'problem' drinking, but they are also reasons for 'social' drinking.[1]

Established conventions of drinking and pub-going can also be problematic for women. Women have consistently told me that they feel pressure to drink — but disapproval if they get drunk. Visiting the pub is one of the most popular forms of entertainment in Britain, yet pub life traditionally revolves around men. Social drinking *can be* an enjoyable and relaxing activity. But all too often for women, the sexism of our society permeates even to the pint.

WHY DO WE DRINK?

Most of us drink because we enjoy it. We like alcohol's mellowing, relaxing effect, we like the convivial social ritual of drinking with friends.

Kate: I love drinking. Many of the best times of my life have been associated with drink — either in celebration of good things happening, or as the result of drink as a catalyst, making things happen.

Drinking is especially important to me as a way of *really talking* with my friends. In a good session over a bottle of whisky all sorts of important things are said that wouldn't be otherwise. It brings you closer to people, creates a greater understanding and intimacy with friends which is tremendously valuable.

I think that women are more creative this way than men. When the men that I know get together for a booze-up the level of their communication doesn't go deeper than usual — they generally don't talk about themselves so much, or about how they feel. For women it seems to be much more an occasion for breaking down barriers and renewing relationships.

And many women, as well as men, look forward to a few drinks as a way of unwinding after a hard day. They regard it positively, as one of the best ways to help themselves cope with the stresses of living in a far from ideal world.

Janet: More than anything else women need to relax. Better to do it on four pints of Special than on a lifetime of tranquillisers.

Lynn: It's a kind of reward. When I've had a really shitty day I promise myself a pint at the end of it. Like yesterday, after driving a hundred miles we were all desperate for a pint. Some of us got really frantic when we thought the pubs had closed at ten-thirty and we were going to be too late.

Sarah: I think there would be an awful lot more suicides in the world if we didn't have drink. Why shouldn't people drink when they have so much to put up with from day to day? I also drink to get things out of myself, a lot of them shitty things that I would like to be able to say anyway, but can't.

Alison: Being on the dole has a lot to do with drinking. Me and a friend were unemployed for about eighteen months. We used to sit at home and drink a couple of bottles of cider a day. We had nothing else to do.

Alex: I would be scared if I couldn't drink ever again. Life would be too bland, too boring.

Diane: I used to drink because I was shy, timid, I had no confidence. I thought I had no brain. I thought I was stupid. Drink gave me confidence to say and do things.

After having children my drinking went down a lot. I had something that was mine. I had love, I had caring. My husband didn't do that for me — to him I was a stray cat that he brought in off the road. Without my children I wouldn't be here today.

But whatever our motives for drinking, and no matter how straight-forward they may seem, inevitably we find ourselves entangled with complex taboos and social pressures.

Lynn: It's a cultural thing. The crowd of people I work with go to the pub at lunchtime and afterwards — it's our habit of socialising.

In certain groups you get an image of being a regular boozer. I am the court jester in my group at work. I'm the one who is expected to make everyone laugh.

If I said I didn't want to go to the pub, or asked for an orange juice, there would be raised eyebrows. It's just not the role I play. They expect me to say, 'Jesus, when's the pub open?' — and everyone goes Ho ho ho. It's a sort of Pavlovian reflex, a kind of shorthand substitute for the conversation that dribbles away through the working day.

Its also a way of *not doing* other things. The big problems of the world and the little problems of your life actually don't seem so ghastly when you've had a few pints. You can blather on about them for a while, get pissed, have a great conversation — and at the same time you are not doing anything about them. You are using up time. It's like the song about 'When the pub closes the revolution starts ...'

But if you don't drink you are a constant reminder to others that your behaviour is really more sensible than everyone else's. Other people who are getting pissed feel a real antagonism if you don't. It's guilt.

Maggie: There's a huge social pressure to drink. You've *got* to have one. Its really difficult to ask for an orange juice, especially with people from work. It's just not accepted.

Sarah: I'm Irish and I've always had a reputation for being a drinker. At times I feel a pressure that I've got to live up to it.

There have been times when I've got drunk from desperation, but I feel happier with my drinking patterns now — except I feel a lot of guilt about wasted days when I drink too much on Friday nights.

Sarah is certainly not alone in feeling guilt about drinking. This sense that women 'should' be responsible about not wasting time has its basis in the prescribed female role of homemaker and child rearer.

Not only is drinking likely to make a woman less efficient as a housekeeper but, researchers argue, taboos against women drinking stem from fears that we will cease to be as sensitive and caring to others as we are supposed to be as mothers: 'There is no doubt that excessive drinking of alcohol grossly interrupts the sensitivity to the needs of others [which] is the essential feature of the second part of the female role — that of child rearer.'[2]

The sexual division of labour and women's traditional role in the family are at the root of social taboos against women's drinking, internalised in us as confusion and guilt.

This awareness that drinking is conventionally regarded as a 'bad thing' in women goes together with a fear of losing control which stops many women from getting drunk.

Janet: The reason why a lot of women don't drink so much as men is that they're frightened of losing control. I'm a teacher and at the end of term I feel I really want to get pissed, just to think of something other than work.

But women have got kids to look after, meals to prepare, hundreds of little things to do. Even for someone like me who doesn't have kids there's always something to do, like the washing or the cleaning. I can't just lie in bed like a man can lie in bed. I've got to get up and do things. I can't waste the whole tomorrow.

It was also drilled into me by my mother not to waste time. She told me that, as a woman, it was an absolute shame for me to waste a day lying in bed with a hangover.

So you don't lose control. You go just far enough and no further.

The strong disapproval of drunkenness affects Black women in much the same way.

Jean: Bars in our culture are for men. It is frowned upon for Black women to go to pubs; it is seen as the English way of life.

In the West Indies where my family comes from, men go to the bars. But women will drink socially at home. My mother makes punch, often out of Guinness, when we have visitors, but I have never seen her or any of her women friends drunk.

I would be looked down on socially if I got drunk. Men would look down on a woman who drank too much.

Marjorie: The things that once stopped white women from drinking are still stopping Black women. We don't use alcohol apart from socially. It is virtually unknown to us to have 'a good time' on alcohol — we have 'a good time' dancing or at parties. We don't seek release in alcohol either. We bear the problem, or have a moan to a friend.

For a Black woman to be alcoholic is a terrible additional stigma. It means you are in a minority of a minority of a minority.

And we can't afford to go around being drunk.

Another factor which puts women off drinking to excess is that being drunk leaves us with lowered defences against harassment.

Maggie: After socialising in the pub I usually have to go home on my own on the tube or the bus. For men it's okay. No one is going to bother them. But for a woman it's bad enough at night anyway, and if your vision is blurred and you're a bit queasy then you are much more vulnerable to being attacked. That stops me from getting out of control.

Being out of control — and not *under* control — has other social dangers for women. 'We don't like our women to drink. They become uncontrollable,' writes a buyer for an off-licence chain in *Marketing Week Magazine*. Much of the depression and guilt which all too often come with hangovers stem from a sense of embarrassment or shame that last night we behaved in an 'unfeminine' fashion.

Lynn: The image of the pissed man is very different from that of the pissed woman. The bloke who goes out, gets legless, falls over, goes to sleep on the train, misses his stop and has to walk miles home at three o'clock in the morning is a 'good laugh', 'one of the lads'. He's got a good story to tell in the office the next morning.

Now a woman who does that is not seen in the same way *at all*. It's not a great story — it's a little bit ... distasteful. It's not a joke. A woman who gets into a right old state and falls over, *she's* not a folk hero. There's definitely a double standard.

Maggie: And, for women, the image of spending a 'night on the tiles' immediately takes on a sexual connotation. For men the reality is just the opposite — they can't perform at all.

This idea that drink makes women sexually 'promiscuous' is a common and deep-rooted one, despite the lack of evidence for it. 'One who tips off the liquor with an appetite and exclaims good, good, by a smack of her lip, is fit for nothing but a brothal, 'wrote William Cobbett in the eighteenth century.

Are male fears of impotence from the dreaded 'brewers' droop' projected on to drinking women, so that the blame becomes ours as creatures of voracious sexual appetite?

IN THE PUB

Nowhere in the social sphere is the drinking double-standard so evident — yet so much taken for granted — as in that great bastion of British social life, the pub.

More than two-thirds of the adult population go to a pub at least once a year, according to *Brewing Review* (autumn 1981), the Brewers' Society journal which published results of a MORI investigation into the public's drinking habits. This makes the pub the most popular leisure pursuit in the country apart from TV-watching, and ranks it ahead of eating out, going dancing and going to the cinema. Nearly a third of the British public goes to the pub once a week.

Yet going to the pub is a different experience for most women that it is for men.

Lynn: I feel I'm an oddity — a woman, in a pub, if I am by myself. I need a prop, another reason for being there. So I buy the *Standard*. I hate the bloody *Standard* — but it makes it seem like I've gone in there not to have a drink but to sit and read the paper. I need that prop between me and those men standing at the bar. They're not oddities; they're in their own world.

I like going into the pub at lunchtime for a pint and a sandwich, but in the evening there is more of a sexual threat if you are on your own. To have someone else with you makes you feel more secure. Going in with another woman is a sort of more interesting version of the *Standard*.

This feeling of vulnerability, of being regarded as sexually available, is a common complaint amongst women who drink in pubs — whether aone or with friends.

Linda: I always feel hassled if I go into a pub with women friends. Perhaps the men feel threatened by us. I have a friend who is very sexy and an excellent pool player. When she goes into pubs the men just look at her and say, 'Coooor ...' They don't take her seriously — until she starts beating them at pool.

Amrit: I never go alone into a pub. The men look at you as if they think you are a prostitute, they all look round, it's horrible. Or they try to pick you up.

Yvonne: I hate waiting for people in a pub. It's a hostile environment. I feel as if it's a man's place to be, and as a woman alone I stick out. It's not just that people will be trying to chat you up, but that they will probably be thinking, 'Oh, poor woman, on her own.'

Stephanie: I just don't feel comfortable going into a pub on my own. I once waited in the toilet for a quarter of an hour for a friend to arrive.

I used to go home to Southend at weekends and go into the pub to see the local crowd. But my confidence would evaporate as I walked in as I always felt other people criticised me for being on my own, as if I had come there to pick someone up.

Perhaps it is because we are often made to feel ill at ease that nearly half of women drinkers establish a familiar pub. Forty-three per cent of women pub goers use a 'regular' compared with 51 per cent of men.

But this high figure for women with regulars (from the Brewer's Society/MORI poll) could be deceptive. It seems to imply that nearly as many women as men have a pub where they can meet friends and feel at home. Yet all too often women's drinking habits are dictated by the men they associate with. A woman will inherit a new 'regular' with a new man, and when the relationship breaks up she disappears from the scene, losing contact with the whole social group.

Susan: I started going to pubs when I was fifteen with my elder brothers and their mates. I continued drinking with male friends and lovers — in the places which served *their* favourite beer. I have spent up to a year going to a boyfriend's local, getting to know the bar staff, making friends with the other regulars — and then the relationship ends, and that's *it*. I never go into *his* pub again, never meet those people again.

My father thought it was great that I went out drinking with men. It proved to him that I was popular, not a 'wallflower'. And the standard way for any of my boyfriends to get his approval was to bring him a bottle of whisky when they came to visit. He used to say that his main worry was that his daughters would marry dreadful men — the type who wouldn't go out for a drink with him.

Men can have a strong influence over women's drinking habits. Men's heavy drinking often starts when they are young and drinking with their peers. But women's alcohol problems usually develop when they are older — in their thirties or forties — and are often the result of their husbands' or men friends' influence.[3] Women alcoholics are well known to have a greater rate than men of parental alcoholism, and they often marry men with alcohol problems.

But for some women moving into the traditionally male arena of the pub is an attempt to assert their independence from men and from the home, and a chance to break their social isolation.

Sarah: I love going down to my local, meeting women, drinking and talking. I think it is a real liberation for women to be able to escape from the confines of home. No amount of publicity about the risks of drinking for women is going to make me go back home again.

The Canning is *my* local, not one I go to because my boyfriend does, which is usually the case for women.

Once in the pub, patterns of drinking are again different for men and women. Most men drink beer, usually bitter, and drink more of it than women.

Brewing Review (autumn 1981) reports that 86 per cent of the men interviewed in their survey drank beer. More than half of these drank more than two pints per visit to the pub, and more than a third drank three to four pints.

By contrast, less than a third (29 per cent) of the women interviewed preferred beer. Most of those opted for lager, and rarely consumed more than two pints at a time. Only about one in ten of beer drinking women will have three to four pints on a visit. The majority of women choose to drink spirits (33 per cent), wine and sherry (24 per cent), or soft drinks (24 per cent).

Of course there are great regional variations in the social codes about women drinking, and women in the south of England and London generally say that they feel more at ease than women from the north do in pubs. And in many places considerable prejudice persists against women drinking pints, an 'unfeminine' drink — in type and quantity.

A Scottish survey showed that both drinking and drunkenness were viewed less favourably in women than in men.[4] Most men (90 per cent) and even more women (93 per cent) thought that the sight of a drunken woman was far more disgusting than that of a drunken man. And half of the women (49 per cent) thought it was degrading for a woman to be seen drinking in a pub — even more than the men who disapproved.

Janet: In the north, women still don't go into pubs in the backwater areas. A couple of months ago I was at home in Yorkshire and when I ordered a pint of beer it came in two half-pint glasses.

Anny: And isn't it ridiculous — the 'ladies' glasses' syndrome where they give you beer in glasses with stems like wine glasses if you are a woman?

Elaine: If my mother saw me drinking pints she would be really shocked — yet it's perfectly okay for me to drink a double vodka and tonic.

Kate: I'm from Bolton and men at home are really surprised when they offer to buy me a drink and I ask for half of lager or half of bitter. They expect me to ask for a Pina Colada or something fancy like that.

I let them buy drinks for me because I know that they have got more money than me, and probably wouldn't accept drinks from me if I did offer.

The business of buying drinks, with all its complexities of social etiquette is another area of pub custom where women frequently run into difficulties. If you do let a man buy all the drinks you will probably pay with the uncomfortable feeling that you owe him something, or that *he* feels you owe him something — socially and/or sexually.

Even when the element of obligation is submerged, the sense of patronage and of the man's superior economic power remains strong. Like the 'gentleman' who opens doors for 'ladies', he feels that he is acting correctly and it would be churlish of you to refuse. You know that he is acting 'correctly' — and that's the trouble — chivalry is all too often a disguise for dominance.

In working relationships, these social codes can be especially stifling for women when a male colleague or boss pays for all the drinks. The woman is placed in the position of guest to the man as host. She feels indebted while he exercises control. In drinking situations with a male colleague or boss who has, at least, the power of hire and fire over her, a woman will find it doubly difficult to assert herself.

More and more women do now pay their own way in pubs — which is not to say they have no further problems.

Lynn: Getting served is terrible. It makes me so angry. You are waiting there at the bar holding out your fiver and a man behind you shouts out, 'A couple of pints please' — and no problem, he gets served before you.

Janet: And women barmaids are worse than men. They always serve the men first. They look right through me as if to say, 'Go and sit down, dear, this isn't your place, you should be cooking the dinner.' It really infuriates me.

This disapproval of women by women has serious consequences in intensifying the isolation of women with drink problems, but it must be seen in context. It is not surprising that women should absorb and reflect the 'moral' strictures which permeate the dominant — and misogynist — culture, especially since we are the ones that risk the brunt of social disapproval.

Nor is the widely practised round system as fair to women who want to buy drinks as it might seem.

Liz: I never had much money so I used to drink half pints of beer. But I would always rush up to the bar to buy a round because I wanted to pay my way equally. Then I realised what a good thing the men had going for them: they always drank pints so I was paying out for more than they were.

So I started drinking pints myself to even things out a bit, but I realised that again I had just adopted a male pattern of drinking — and one that's bad for my health.

We need to progress beyond drinking as 'equals' with men in pubs, to a confidence in our own preferences.

Liz is reacting to a dilemma which is increasingly common for young women drinkers. On the one hand, we face a challenge to live up to vague but misplaced notions of equality, keeping up with men drink for drink, buying round for round. But this is not so much 'equality' as *sameness* with men. Equality is far more complex. Women may not *want* to drink so much, we cannot physically tolerate the same amounts of drink as men, and generally we have less spending money than men. Women cannot simply adopt male patterns of socialising when the conditions of our lives are not the same — and why should we even wish to?

Women with children have particular reason to feel that the prevailing customs of pub life do not cater to their needs, because so few pubs make provision for children.

Anny: The question of women drinking in pubs is a battle that has largely been won. But the idea of a pub for the family is still totally alien. At our local trades council club we are now fighting to get one room used for a children's room.

Now that I have a baby, it's a major operation to go out. You have to make sure the pub has a beer garden — and that's no good except in summer and at lunchtime or early evening. In Europe, going out is far more of a family thing, but in Britain it's very difficult to go anywhere with kids — especially for women who still have the main responsibility for childcare.

It also makes it very difficult for women to get to political meetings which are often held in pubs.

Janet: My father's whole idea in going to the pub was to get away from the family. He used to say, 'I can't stand those screaming kids a moment longer. I'm going to the pub!'

According to *Brewing Review*, there is still very little public support for the idea of providing children's rooms in pubs. As part of the survey, pub goers were asked to choose from a list of features to describe their idea of the 'ideal pub'. Only 26 per cent of women and 18 per cent of men thought 'special facilities for children' were a good idea.

These results no doubt followed from the terms of the survey itself. A woman's choice of features for her 'ideal pub' will probably reflect her notion of what is practicably obtainable *now*. Pubs that welcome children, being about as commons as pubs that serve free drinks, may have been dismissed as an unrealistic goal.

For women, the highest priority turned out to be clean toilets (63 per cent), which are both desirable and obtainable. (Unfortunately the survey didn't ask women how they felt about the usually interminable trek to those toilets — out of the bar, along the corridor, up the stairs, along another corridor ... Women also gave high ratings to friendly bar staff (53 per cent), clean glasses and comfortable seats (52 per cent in both instances).

Men thought these elements were important too, but put more stress on the pub being used by their friends (50 per cent as opposed to 35 per cent of women), which confirms the picture of the pub as predominantly a meeting place for men.

Men more than women wanted the pub to be within walking distance of home (men are more likely to drink themselves above the legal driving limit), and gave higher priority to good beer, dart boards and other games than did women. Twenty per cent of men (as opposed to 2 per cent of women) thought that 'attractive barmaids' were important. (The survey didn't ask whether 'attractive barmen' were important.)

Our preferences for the ideal drinking environment are different from men's, but the traditional pub seems unlikely to change for our sakes — unless it is to clean up its toilets. In the words of a Brewers' Society spokesman, as reported by the *Guardian* (27 July 1982), 'A large number of pubs have something of the air of gentlemen's clubs, and the presence of too many women might spoil that.'

Some pubs still discriminate against women by operating bars exclusively for men, by refusing to serve women pints, and by excluding women from snooker tables and dart boards. This has been against the law since the 1975 Sex Discrimination Act, so if your complaints are ignored, contact the Equal Opportunities Commission.[5]

More and more women are now seeking alternatives to the traditional pub. At least one London pub has found that a weekly women's night was so successful that *every* night is now women's night. The wine bar trade is also booming, not only because many women prefer wine, but as one proprietor put it: 'Women can go into them and be reasonable sure they won't be hassled.' A *Guardian* (27 July 1982) article reports that their popularity results from the 'freedom ... of sitting in a drinking place without being accosted, pinched, chatted up or loudly and anatomically commented on'.

Other women avoid pubs altogether, and abstain on moral or political grounds.

Brenda: I don't drink. I'm not going to touch anything that quietens me down. I want to be really alive. If we were allowed to be as alive as we could be, we could kick alcohol out of the door.

And the organisers of the mass women's peace protest at Greenham Common in December 1982 asked people coming to Greenham on that day not to drink alcohol. They suggested on their leaflets that drinking would be out of keeping with the life-affirming spirit of the occasion.

American feminists have made a film about an alcoholism centre for women called *We All Have Our Reasons* which portrays women's drinking as an explicitly political issue. One woman wears a T-shirt with the slogan 'Alcoholism is a women's issue', and in their group sessions the women talk and laugh and cry about their experiences.

'I drank not to be myself,' says one. 'When I drank I wasn't myself — that made it okay for me to be alive,' says another, who had been told for so long that she was worthless that she came to believe it.

The director of the centre explains that many women are not allowed by society to be who they really are. This denial includes our sexuality, and because of this lesbian women find themselves especially oppressed. 'Women are turning themselves inside out not to be themselves,' she says, 'especially lesbians.'

The film concludes that alcohol is another 'opium of the people'. 'If anyone wanted to diabolically set out to keep a people down,' says a commentator on pictures of down-and-outs comatose on the streets, 'alcohol would be the best possible way. It pacifies them.'

And the film ends on this note: 'Think about the kind of energy kept in women by drinking ... If women were to stop drinking, think where that energy would go. We could change the world.'

A WOMAN'S PLACE

Women have low or no self-esteem; women have extreme feelings of guilt; women experience much depression; women, more often than not, must combat their alcoholism alone, nine out of ten husbands leaving them. There is no male equivalent to the drinking housewife. Women suffer not only from alcoholism but from role identification. Women lack a clear image of their role as women, our culture having created much of the confusion. Women alcoholics feel they have failed as wives, as mothers, as women. They feel guilty because society makes them feel so. All women live in a sexist society.

From a letter written by Jean Kirkpatrick, Ph.D., an alcoholic and counsellor of women alcoholics and President of Women for Sobriety Inc. to Senator William Hathaway

Being a woman drinker — alcoholic or not — is, as the women speaking here have said, a complex and often guilt-ridden business. Women drinkers have already talked about their feelings of failure — as wives, as mothers, as women — and about the contradictory experiences of social drinking: the desire to unwind or escape through alcohol, the fear of losing control, the guilt of drunkenness.

Why does drinking stir up so much confusion and guilt in women? This can only be seen against the background of what women are *expected* to be. In this chapter I look at these expectations as they are reflected in the stereotyped images of women and women drinkers in advertising, books, films and the media. The basic 'given' is that we are valued as mates and mothers, and time and time again the drinking woman is portrayed with hostility and/or disgust as a deviant from that role.

Instead of accepting blame for being 'failures' as women, or guilt for our drinking, let's ask whether we accept the stereotyped images of the 'normal' woman which are projected by our culture?

THE HAND THAT ROCKS THE CRADLE

Drunkenness is popularly thought to be much 'worse' in women than in men (see chapter 2). Joan Curlee, an American authority on alcoholism in women, explains it like this:

> Because the role of woman has been equated with the stabilising functions of wife and mother, the drunken woman is seen to be a special threat; no one likes to believe that the hand that rocks the cradle might be a shaky one. Even among alcoholic women themselves, it is not unusual to hear this statement: 'There is nothing so disgusting as a drunken woman.'
>
> According to the stereotype a woman who has deserted her feminine role sufficiently to be an alcoholic has deserted respectability in all areas, especially the sexual one. Students of the problem realise that this stereotype is as false as most others, yet it persists.

There are a few examples from history of groups of women who drank heavily. Hogarth's famous Gin Lane print, which shows a child tumbling from the lap of a ragged and dishevelled woman who is drunkenly oblivious to its fate, marks one such era. Significantly, gin was called 'Mother's Ruin'. The print is memorable not simply as an exceptional example of female drunkenness, but because the image of a drunken woman is depicted with horror — and inspires horror.

That sense of horror is still with us. 'Let's face it — there really is nothing manly or heroic about those who drink too much,' said Mr David Ennals, then Secretary of State for Social Services, to the opening of a Health Education campaign. 'In men it is crude and embarrassing: in women it is plain sickening.'

To get drunk is to threaten our prescribed female role and to bring condemnation upon ourselves.

THE 'NORMAL' WOMAN

When Shirley Otto, a research psychologist and founder member of DAWN (Drugs, Alcohol, Women — Nationally), and her colleague Ian Petrie produced a revue for the Camberwell Council on Alcoholism, they chose these three quotations to express some prevailing notions of the feminine role.

> Women are usually more patient in working at unexciting, repetitive tasks. Women on average have more passivity in the

inborn core of their personality. I believe women are designed in their deeper instincts to get more pleasure out of life — not only sexually, but socially, occupationally, maternally — when they are not aggressive. To put it another way I think that when women are encouraged to be competitive, too many of them become disagreeable.

The fact of the matter is that the prime responsibility of a woman probably is to be on earth long enough to find the best male possible for herself, and conceive children who will improve the species.

To one (woman) belongs the power of feeling, the power of the soul, to the other (man) belongs the strength of vision, the strength of hardness. The man upholds the nation as the woman upholds the family.

The first quotation comes from Dr Benjamin Spock, whose influence extended over a whole generation of western mothers and babies. The second comes from the novelist and critic Norman Mailer, and the third is from Adolf Hitler.

Each expresses a stereotype of women — that is, an oversimplified but widely held view about what the typical woman is. They each believe that our role is to be passive and non-competitive, that our place is in the home as spouse and child rearer — and that women are *born* with these sets of characteristics.

You may not have considered Spock, Mailer and Hitler to have been in the same stream of modern thought, but the sex-role stereotypes which they express are pervasive and powerful, embodying lasting and deeply felt prejudices. One such prejudice is that women are not 'healthy' or 'adult' in the same way that men are. When workers in the mental health field were asked to chose adjectives which described a healthy adult,[1] they came up with words which generally matched their ideas of what a *man* should be. But the characteristics attributed by them to a healthy woman — sensitivity, dependence and self-centredness — were more like those we associate with a child.

And together with this notion of women not being fully adult goes the idea that we are somehow irresponsible 'by nature' — and so in need of control. Bridget Hutter and Gillian Williams have explored the many definitions of what it means to be 'normal' or 'deviant' in our society.[2] They find 'the image of the "normal" woman is ... time and time again ... of a person with something of a childish incapacity to govern herself and in some need of protection — a kind of original sin stemming from Eve's inability to control her desire to seek new knowledge'.

THE SOCIAL REALITY — 'BRUTE INEQUALITIES'

This supposed incapacity of women is mirrored in our inferior social position. In 1982 the Advertising Standards Authority published their study of images of women in advertisements, *Herself Appraised*, which assessed the current status of women.

The ASA, which is the advertising industry watchdog, may seem an odd source for information about women's social position, but I have used it precisely because it is in this industry's interest to have the clearest possible idea of the status quo and of the directions of change in our society. And because it is this industry which profits by projecting images of us as women and as drinkers, advertising, says the report, 'cannot but reflect the character of the economy and the society which sustains it'.

To gauge this character, the ASA looked back to Victorian times and concluded that, until the 1950s at least, the campaign for women's liberation had 'largely secured its aims'. But the ASA recognised that 'formal legal equality' was not enough to confront the 'brute inequalities of the labour market':

> British society asserts the desirability of formal legal equality between the sexes, but has not yet assimilated its consequences for a labour market which women must enter, leave and re-enter in accordance with the requirements of family building. In these circumstances equality remains a distant goal, the achievement of which must wait upon society's ability and willingness to draw out the consequences of the new relationship between motherhood and work which became widely visible in the early 1960s.

Even as traditional a body as the ASA recognises the lip service our society has paid to the idea of equality while doing nothing to change the structures of the family or the organisation of paid work which keep women unequal. Our expectations have been raised — and unfulfilled.

On the one hand we feel our role to be changing. In many ways the position of women *has* improved in recent decades: we are now some 40 per cent of the paid labour force, we have more disposable income and more equality before the law. But men still hold power over women, age-old notions of women's innate inferiority maintain their grip and the time-honoured stereotype that 'a woman's place is in the home' persists. No wonder we feel confusion about what we 'should' be as women.

WOMEN DRINKERS: THE POPULAR IMAGE

In all the manifestations of popular culture — in song and story, films, newspapers and television — the most misogynistic elements of the female stereotype become highlighted and exaggerated into the stereotype of the female drinker.

... in fiction: Drunk women and women with drink problems are rare in our literature, but when they do appear it is in a most unflattering light. Women as homeless alcoholics received a particularly bad press in both the scientific and fictional literature reviewed by Shirley Otto. There is, she writes, 'no female equivalent of the noble savage portrayal of the male homeless alcoholic'.[3] While writers such as George Orwell and Jack Kerouac portray male down-and-outs as romantic heroes, 'almost no films or books romanticise the female tramp or hobo; such women really do not excite anyone's fantasy or envy'. This is not to suggest that women drinkers *deserve* a more 'romantic' treatment. What is at issue here is the comparative distaste expressed about women drinkers, *because they are women.*

Yet our literature is chock full of romantic male heroes who drink to extinction. Hemingway's hero in *A Farewell to Arms* drinks his way through love, war and hospital, scoring points over an angry nursing staff (Nagging Women) when they find his hospital locker full of bottles.

Raymond Chandler's novels feature a host of hard-drinking heroes whose alcoholic habits are seen as a natural adjunct to their macho personalities. Alternatively, alcohol helps Chandler's more 'sensitive' and romantic characters — like Philip Marlowe — in their struggle to 'bear the pain of existence' and cope with their feelings.

His novel, *The Long Goodbye*, features two alcoholic men, the enigmatic and misunderstood Terry Lennox and the famous author Roger Wade. Both are portrayed sympathetically, both are rescued from alcoholic benders by the considerate Marlowe, and both are the victims of ruthless and/or 'promiscuous' women.

In contrast, drinking women in the novel are portrayed with contempt and revulsion. The following passage combines some classic stereotypes:

> A small girl with mud-coloured hair and a band around her forehead popped up beside me and put a glass on the bar and bleated ...
>
> 'Are you interested in Communism?' she asked me. She was glassy eyed and she was running a small red tongue along her lips as if looking for a crumb of chocolate. 'I think everyone ought to be,' she went on. 'But when you ask any of the men here they just

want to paw you.'

I nodded and looked over my glass at her snub nose and sun-coarsened skin.

'Not that I mind too much if it's done nicely,' she told me, reaching for the fresh drink. She showed me her molars while she inhaled half of it.

The woman asks Marlowe his name, and starts reciting poetry. Then she

put her glass down damn nearly empty and closed her eyes and threw her head back and her arms out, almost hitting me in the eye. Her voice throbbed with emotion ...

'You can kiss me if you like,' she said coyly.

This woman is a photofit package of misogynist stereotypes. She is childish ('small girl'), greedy ('inhaled' her drink), grossly sub-human ('bleated', 'sun-coarsened', 'molars'), sentimental, crass, manipulative — and sexually 'permissive'.

Alcoholic women are commonly seen as *either* sluttish *or* sexless, and there are examples in Chandler of both extremes:

There are blondes and blondes and all blondes have their points ... There is the soft and willing alcoholic blonde who doesn't care what she wears as long as it is mink or where she goes as long as it is the Starlight Roof and there is plenty of dry champagne.

These alcoholic stereotypes are *either* sexy, willing and shameless — *or* ugly, dirty, animalistic and devoid of sexuality. But both of them are greedy, as is this woman who blows her nose

on one of the dirtiest handkerchiefs I ever saw. Her eyes stayed on the bottle. Suspicion fought with thirst, and thirst was winning. It always does ...

Seaweed coloured eyes stayed on the bottle. A coated tongue coiled on her lips ...

I poured her a slug that would have made me float over a wall. She reached for it hungrily and put it down her throat and looked at the bottle.

This aura of disgust clings to female drinking characters even when their portrayal is purportedly sympathetic. Anthony Burgess' book *Beard's Roman Women* has as its central character a middle-aged script writer. To his dismay, his wife, after years of keeping pace with his heavy drinking, has developed cirrhosis of the liver:

He realised too late what should always have been self-evident:

that a woman was a smaller vessel than a man, that no man had a right to expect a woman, however much a woman wished it, to be a real, meaning drink for drink, companion.

(There is a patronising and false assumption that all women would *wish* to follow the male drinking pattern if we could.) For some time their life is 'companionate' — i.e. without sex. Her illness and subsequent death are described in horrible detail with the emphasis on the decay of her 'former beauty', and on how repellent her body becomes as a result of the liver disease.

After her death the 'hero' finds himself involved in a string of sexual adventures with young and 'sexy' women. His wife has paid for her drinking with her life, while he is released to a fantasy life of rejuvenated sexual activity and freedom.

Male writers — as characters and as authors — often do have reputations as drinkers which enhance rather than detract from their images. Figures like Brendan Behan and Dylan Thomas are legendary for their drinking exploits. Scott Fitzgerald was also said to have enjoyed the romantic interest which surrounded him as a 'man who drank'. Yet when he wrote to the doctor looking after his wife Zelda,[4] then in a mental hospital, he blamed her bad example for his own drinking:

I gave my wife a comfortable and luxurious life such as few European writers ever achieve ... My work is done on coffee, coffee and more coffee, never on alcohol. At the end of five or six hours I get up from my desk white and trembling and with a steady burn in my stomach to go to dinner.

Doubtless a certain irritability developed in those years, an inability to be gay, which my wife — who had never tried to use her talents and intelligence — was not inclined to condone. It was on our coming to Europe in 1924 and upon her urging that I began to look forward to wine at dinner — she took it at lunch, I did not. We went on hard drinking parties together sometimes, but the regular use of wine and aperitives was something that I dreaded but she encouraged because she found I was more cheerful then and allowed her to drink more.

The ballet idea was something I inaugurated in 1927 to stop her idle drinking after she had already so lost herself in it as to make suicidal attempts. Since then I have drunk more, from unhappiness, and she less, because of her physical work — that is another story.

The judgements Fitzgerald makes in this letter parallel those that

Shirley Otto found to be typical in her review of the literature: that women who drink too much are immature, compulsive, masochistic, passive, and wilfully destroying themselves rather than taking control of the situation. In contrast, Fitzgerald justifies his drinking as a relief from the strain of creativity — drinking in men is often associated with creativity, talent and self-expression — and from 'unhappiness', for which Zelda is to blame. The implication is that she has 'driven him to drink'.

And many of the books written about alcohol itself perpetuate the old stereotypes about men and women drinkers. This story is intended to illustrate the dreadful things that can happen when a drinker has a blackout, but the anecdote serves better as an illustration of the deep misogyny which informs our whole culture — and our attitudes to drinking:

> A man wakes up in a hotel room with an appalling hangover to find, sleeping peacefully beside him, an extremely ugly woman. He groans, gets out of bed quietly, dresses, puts twenty pounds on the bedside table and is starting to walk out when he feels a tug at his trouser leg. He looks down and sees a woman who is even uglier than the one in bed. She gazes up at him and says, 'How about something for the bridesmaid?'[5]

The man in this parable got drunk and became the victim of female seduction and entrapment in marriage. It is a warning to men of what can happen when the usual stereotype — of man seducing willing drunk woman — is reversed. His fate is to be married to 'an extremely ugly woman'. (And anyway, 'there's no fun screwing a drunken broad', according to one male interviewee in the same book, 'even if she's your wife.')

The drunken bridegroom anecdote belongs to a long tradition of stories about men getting drunk together. The earliest recorded stories of Old English celebrate Anglo-Saxon heroes who swilled back the ale while recounting their exploits of fights with monsters, and/or fights with other men. Women make rare appearances in these tales as bearers of drinking cups, or objects of battle.

In medieval England, John Skelton wrote a long narrative poem, 'The Tunning of Elynour Rumming', describing the women who came to drink the brew of Elynour ('sometimes she blends/the dung of her hens ...'):

> Some wenches come unlased
> Some huswives come unbrased [undone]
> With their naked pappes [breasts]
> That flippes and flappes
> It wigges and it wagges

> Like tawney saffron bagges
> A sorte of foule drabbes
> All scurvy with scabbes
> Some be fly bitten
> Some skewed as a kitten
> Some with a sho-clout
> Binde their heddes about
> Some have no here lace
> Their lockes aboute their face
> Their tresses untrussed
> All full of unlust [repulsiveness]

To Skelton's imagination, this group of women drinkers have abandoned all feminine propriety and have sunk to the level of animals.

Yet most of us will have heard boastful stories from contemporary drinking sessions — at sports clubs or stag nights where 'animal' behaviour is the norm. There are few modern female equivalents, apart from the disparagingly named 'hen' party. ('Hen' and 'stag' couldn't be in greater contrast.) In America some younger women have adopted the stag night tradition and get drunk on the night before a wedding. But that the spirit of the occasion is originally masculine is clear from its name — 'bachelorette party'.

... in songs, film and television: in songwriting too it is men, not women, who have recourse to the bottle, either for celebration or for the drowning of sorrows — usually caused by a fickle and faithless woman. There are plenty of love-lorn, heartbroken women in popular songs as well, but they don't sing about getting drunk. It is hard to imagine, say, Carly Simon or Sheena Easton singing, 'Tonight, the bottle let me down,' as Elvis Costello does. Or to imagine Dana or Petula Clark singing, 'The only time I feel all right is when I've been a drinkin',/It eases off the pain a bit and levels out my thinkin',' as the Fury Brothers do.

Nor are there many feature films with a heroine who has drinking problems. In a study of film portrayals of women alcoholics,[6] only one film, *Key Largo*, was found which showed a woman alcoholic as in any way 'heroic' — by the film makers' standards. (I am not implying that it is desirable to portray more women alcoholics in films, or to portray more women alcoholics more 'heroically'; this would only be to mimic the macho pattern.)

These researchers found that films, like books, represented two stereotypes of women alcoholics: 'They are shown either as sluts totally devoid of any self-respect, or as pathetic homeless women.' On the one hand are sexy, cocktail-drinking characters like Mrs Robinson of *The*

Graduate. She seduces the much younger graduate who then rejects her 'embarrassing' advances and marries her daughter. On the other is Edna, *The Inebriate Woman,* pathetic, homeless — and sexless.

When Shirley Otto and her colleagues examined the characteristics of women alcoholics in films, they came up with this list of most common attributes, which are, as Otto points out, 'not much different from those traditionally associated with feminine behaviour':[7]

immature (i.e. never leaves home)	determined
tormented	uses her sexuality for recognition, not pleasure
given to forming destructive relationships	warm
passive	sensitive
masochistic	exploitable
narcissistic	compulsive
uses others to escape/be happy	greedy
	hedonistic
	once beautiful

By contrast, many films portray male alcoholics in a positive, even heroic, light[8] and when — very occasionally — films are made about women with drink problems, they are likely to meet with a horrified reaction like this *Daily Mail* critic's:

> In one field I think women would do well to avoid equality with men. I have in mind alcoholism. There is something formidable and tragic about any alcoholic, but the female variety is really terrible. Nothing more fatally draws attention to this than a film having as its heroine a lush.

In contrast, films like *Animal House,* which shows groups of young men involved in a life of drinking and general debauchery, are greeted as highly comical. Many male comics on film and television get enormous mileage from stories of outrageous drinking sessions. Billy Connolly is famous for his jokes about vomiting drunks (always male). W.C. Fields was a classic alcoholic comedian. Television personalities like Dean Martin and Dave Allen always have a drink to hand — unimaginable for Esther Rantzen or Angela Rippon. Female characters in television shows are less likely to be witty and jovial as drinkers, than sentimental lushes — like Sue Ellen of *Dallas* (she has elements of the sexy, 'promiscuous' stereotype too). And when a 'normal' television star like Yootha Joyce of the domestic series *George and Mildred* dies, 'a victim of alcoholism', according to the *Newcastle-Upon-Tyne Journal,* 'the reaction of her public was a shocked and frozen disbelief'.

... in public and private life: In public life too, a reputation for being a drinker is unlikely to do a man much harm, and may even enhance his reputation as a man of the world who can 'hold his drink'. Winston Churchill was said to be proud of his drinking in the knowledge that it increased his personal reputation and power. The author of a new book on Churchill told the *Standard* that

> a lot of people still think he was a heavy drinker, whereas the truth is he was an eccentric drinker. He would have a scotch and soda at breakfast, yes, but it was a weak one which would last him through lunch ... He encouraged people to think he consumed large quantities of liquor. It was part of his macho image. But he didn't get drunk.

Churchill was said to have doubted that Britain would ever have a woman Prime Minister, but kept an 'open mind'. We now have a woman PM — but imagine if news got out of Mrs Thatcher downing a whisky at breakfast? It wouldn't enhance her image one bit. Thatcher, by contrast, is reputed to make one whisky last all evening while keeping a stern eye on husband Denis' consumption.

And the anecdote of mutual insult which is said to have passed between Churchill and Margot Asquith shows how easily a man can shake off an accusation of drunkenness. Again, 'ugliness' is his weapon of attack —

Margot Asquith: 'Mr Churchill, you are drunk.'

Winston Churchill: 'And you, madam, are ugly, but I shall be sober tomorrow.'

Churchill is putting down a woman who is telling him off for being drunk, and here we have another well-worn stereotype, the Nagging Woman. Her image is so common that we take it for granted. Andy Capp escapes Flo's fury by going down to the pub; Stanley retreats from Hilda Ogden to *Coronation Street's* Rover's Return. 'A woman drove me to drink, and I never even thanked her for it,' quipped W.C. Fields, drawing on the same stereotype.

The assumption behind this is that, for men, it is understandable, natural and justifiable to seek solace from emotional discomfort in alcohol, and that women's unreasonable demands are the source of this discomfort. Again, there is no parallel assumption about women's needs for solace. 'Men drink to drown their sorrows, women drink to revive them,' goes an old saw told to me by my father. When women *do* turn to drink, the assumption is not that we need relief from emotional pain, but that we are drinking from perversity and spite, causing our men embarrassment and shame.

Female Alcoholics[9] gives the following as one of a number of reasons for the increase in women's drinking suggested by 'authorities in the alcohol field': 'Some female drinking is motivated by spite, simply to "get at" husbands who may not spend enough time with their families.' Some women, it continues, have a 'spiteful' attitude towards their drinking husbands, stating that they felt 'what was good for their husbands was good for them'.

Yet the same report gives this as the background to these women's drinking:

> 'Among the women, domestic stress was the most commonly reported reason for their drinking. In men, a difficult work situation was most often given. Significantly more of the women had an alcoholic spouse.' The women also suffered more from depressive illnesses than the men which often 'antedated the onset of their drinking. The women also more frequently claimed an unhappy childhood, which suggested they were liable to be hurt by subsequent stresses.'

The same text is at once acknowledging the misery and desperate position of these women, *and* 'blaming the victim'. By putting their drinking down to 'spite' it implies that the women are guilty of moral failures in their vindictiveness and lack of tolerance.

Another reason suggested by the 'authorities' for the increase in women's drinking, says the report, is the 'advent of "women's lib" '. Our greater freedom is 'leading to more wives joining their partners in the public house or even *venturing in alone*' (my italics). This is a logic based on the stereotype of Eve 'in need of protection' and with a 'childish incapacity to govern herself'.

... in the news: The media reflect and perpetuate such attitudes. This is how the *Guardian* reported a conference on alcoholism:

> A doctor said evidence showed that many alcoholics had taken to drink because of their wives' behaviour. 'But we are now finding that more and more women are turning to alcohol to drown their sorrows, brought on by their alcoholic husbands,' he added. 'These married women probably do it to get their own back on their husbands and perhaps feel that they are paying him back for the sorrow he has brought them.'[10]

The inference is that husbands turn to drink because of their wives' behaviour, while wives turn to drink because of their husbands' behaviour — *and* 'probably ... to get their own back'. I have yet to come across a suggestion that men drink from vengeance or spite.

And wearisome stereotypes of women and women drinkers appear in feature articles like this one from the *Newcastle-Upon-Tyne Journal*. Entitled 'Mother's Ruin', it resounds with moral censure and disgust at drinking women: 'A woman who tries to keep up with the lads, who takes equality to its outer limits and stands her round in the pub, is no lady — in anybody's eyes.' Pubs should not be allowed to become family centres, argues the article, quoting the then director of the National Council on Alcoholism: 'Such a move would mean more women drinkers with problems,' he tells us, and 'a drunken woman has no sophistication'.

And a local publican describes women who are 'like tramps' because of drink, 'easy prey' to the men who top up their drinks 'to ensure they'll get their own way'. 'A drunken woman is violent, aggressive, abusive and totally unreasonable,' he concludes.

The article goes on to describe the 'walking nightmare' of a man whose (first) wife was an alcoholic:

> I was working my guts out to bring home the money for her to go out and spend it on drink ... Imagine when she won't get up out of bed in the morning, when she's screaming abuse and can't stand up and when the kids are having to make excuses for the woman who can't be a proper mother because she's drunk.

All the stereotypes which induce guilt and shame in women drinkers and stigmatise women alcoholics are present in this piece. The drinking women is 'no lady', has 'no sophistication', is a bad mother, is aggressive, is 'easy prey' — sexually permissive and passive.

No doubt a great deal of grief has been suffered by the family in this story, but note that the focus of the ex-husband's anger is his wife's inability to fulfil her role as 'proper mother', for which she is morally to blame. Yet nine out of ten husbands leave their alcoholic wives, while only one out of ten wives leaves their alcoholic husbands. [11]

A *Sunday Press* article echoes the notion that 'ladylike' women value their face and figure — assets which ladies of power, beauty and fame would never jeopardise by boozing entitled 'What Cocktails Do to You', the article publishes a list of mixed drinks and their calories:

> Weight apart, spirits don't do a thing for your skin. You won't see Jackie Kennedy or Grace Kelly holding a brandy, or gin and tonic — champagne perhaps or wine ... Finally, and most important — how does alcohol affect your behaviour? I think that women in particular should honestly consider this point.

But when women are portrayed for male delectation, as in the *Sun's* page three, the double standards come though loud and clear. The headline over one topless model was:

> Spirited Davina's a tonic! A drinking man's dream ... The 21-year-old Lancashire hot pot used to be a barmaid but she would never call time on fun ... And there are no half measures with our spirited page three smasher. Davina loves lively lads who are lager [sic] than life!

This is the ideal woman for the drinking man; young and beautiful, she serves *him* drink and never nags at him to stop.

On the same page is a contemporary Boozy Bridegroom story headed 'Nineteen whiskies nearly killed groom Tony ... Boozy bridegroom Tony Taylor will totter down the aisle today with the world's biggest hangover ... after a lunchtime drink with the lads that nearly killed him.' Tony, who drank nineteen whiskies and two pints in half an hour, 'collapsed in a coma ... and missed his own stag night'.

In contrast to the jokey tone of these *Sun* stories about men's drinking exploits is a piece in the *Standard* headlined, 'Woman Who Drank Eighteen Pints a Day'. 'A woman who drinks up to eighteen pints of lager a day pleaded for her freedom at the Old Bailey today,' the story begins, as if drinking were the crime 'blonde Suzanne' was being tried for. Only towards the end of the story does it become clear that the woman was charged with common assault — while her boyfriend was found guilty of manslaughter, fatally attacking a diplomat in the street while *he*, the boyfriend, was drunk.

... in advertising: Advertising is an industry which deliberately uses stereotype images for purposes of profit. Its aim is to create desire in the consumer for, in this case, a brand of alcohol, by linking the brand with images of the 'ideal', the wished-for world.

Images of women as objects of desire, idealised as young, beautiful and usually white are used to sell alcohol to men. And images of sophisticated, glamorous, wealthy women in the company of 'desirable' males are used to sell alcohol to women.

But advertisers have this dilemma: We have seen that drunkenness is incompatible with notions of the 'normal' female role, and advertisers must carefully skirt the spouse/child rearer areas of stereotyped womanhood to avoid all undesirable suggestions that alcohol makes women, and mothers, drunk.

The advertisers' response is to select certain images of women and to project only those fragments which suit their sales pitch. Whatever is fashionable in modern ideas of liberation is adopted to attract young women drinkers; whatever is 'threatening' in feminism is absent.

The resulting fetishistic images which bombard our conscious and unconscious selves from television and films, billboards and hoardings, newspapers and magazines, confirm both the drinking double standard and the sexual/social double standard:

— Women may drink, but may not get drunk.
— Females 'should' be young and beautiful, objects of male desire.

Advertisers have even managed to capitalise on the fact that drinking is not as acceptable in women as it is in men. They have taken hold of the status quo and turned it to their advantage by suggesting that drinking is something daring and adventurous, a challenge not to be refused by any young, beautiful and fashionably 'liberated' woman: 'Free the Spirit', say the advertisers of Pernod; 'Be tempted', suggest the makers of vodka in campaigns clearly directed at women. One vodka ad shows a bright snake coiled around a cocktail glass. This is a glamorous (and phallic) Garden of Eden image of the excitement of the forbidden, the sophistication of knowledge. But it is quite split off from the image of the 'fallen' Eve, chastised and subjected to man's control.

Yet men's dominion over women *is* Paradise according to one White Horse whisky ad showing a tiny desert island covered with the prone bodies of leggy models in black bikinis. One male, a James Bond look-alike with his trousers shorn off castaway style at the knees, sits at the edge of the island, smugly sipping his drink.

Complaints to the ASA that this ad was offensive to women were not upheld, but women retaliated with a graffiti campaign, obliterating the man from the picture, painting a feminist symbol and writing 'Paradise' on the all-female island which remained.

Many alcohol ads — like this White Horse poster — identify consumption of alcohol with consumption of women's bodies, a common theme in pornography and in slang which describes women in terms of food — meat, crumpet, tasty.

'The only *body* that *satisfies* [my italics] the Grousebeaters' is the slogan of a McEwan's lager cartoon. This depicts a woman in a bikini. Her mouth, breasts and hips are exaggerated. She is supposedly modelling for a painting, but on the easel is a picture of a pint of McEwans. Two men, pop-eyed, tongues hanging out, leer in the direction of the woman's/the pint's *body*. Again, the ASA did not uphold complaints that this advertisement was offensive to women.

Women are increasingly important as consumers in the drinks market, and advertisers have appropriated fashionable notions of 'women's lib' to sell traditionally male drinks to women: 'Why should men have all the serious drinks?' begins a Lowenbrau Pils advertisement:

It has long been an unfortunate tradition that while men cooled themselves with a refreshing beer, the ladies sipped sticky green drinks with cherries ... And if you did want a more sensible drink you were limited to lagers or halves of bitter.

The copy is illustrated by a picture of a young, slim, sophisticated woman sipping from a stemmed, half-pint glass. The advertisement pretends to debunk the old fashioned 'sipped sticky green drinks' stereotype but has merely updated it. And the woman's image suggests that you can drink (high alcohol) beer without getting fat and without being 'unfeminine'.

The copy continues in an arch, conspiratorial tone — Lowenbrau's brewing process takes place

exclusively in Bavaria ... as the men will confirm. (Being very surprised that you know more about Pils than they do!) ... And while they (the German brewers) know that men are critical of beer, they know that the ladies can be positively withering. So Lowenbrau Pils has been brewed very much with that in mind. Because the Germans take their women even more seriously than their beer.

The flattery is supposedly directed at women's superior judgement and criticism. But it consists of patronising suggestions that 'ladies' are 'equal' to challenging male expertise on beer, reducing the concept of equality to the most banal level.

Not all advertisements for alcohol are as blatant as this in their manipulation of stereotyped feminine roles. I studied the ASA's file of advertisements for alcohol which appeared in the print media in the first quarter of 1982. Of a total of 159 advertisements, the great majority used images which were *not* overtly sexual.

But of the remainder which did use directly masculine/feminine imagery the most common technique was to glamorise certain fragments of the 'normal' woman into the 'ideal' woman, associating alcohol with sexual attractiveness and success in finding a desirable (i.e. wealthy, handsome, male) partner.

Red lips and red nails are taken time and again as feminine symbols to suggest that sexy/sophisticated young women drink Babycham, Bulmer's cider and pomagne, Gordon's gin and Power's whisky. One Chantre brandy advertisement shows a woman's lips kissing the bottle — with more than a hint of phallic imagery. The Power's ad includes a woman's lips, a man's hand, and a stereo tuning knob — linking whisky with sexual success and affluence.

Courtship — of the woman by the man — is another popular theme for alcohol advertisers. Courvoisier depict a young Napoleonic officer, eyes closed and lips parted in passionate entreaty, whispering into the ear of a beautiful courtier. She raises a gloved hand to hide her coy smile, tickled pink by his proposition.

'Friendship grows with a Bush', reads a Bushmills advertisement, depicting entwined male and female hands. 'I've a liking for a Viking', says a smiling young woman in a lager advertisement as she lifts a half-pint glass to her lips — again linking sexual satisfaction with alcoholic satisfaction.

Martini use an image of a glass slipper filled with ice cubes, drawing on the age-old Cinderella myth: poor and powerless female is rescued from drudgery by powerful, princely male.

Prinz Kobold table wine appeals to the same pairing-off imperative: 'This lady will never be left on the shelf,' runs the copy beneath a picture of the bottle and a single orchid. Again, wine and woman are identified: this bottle will always be in demand — as an attractive woman should be.

Idyllic coupledom is the theme of a number of advertisements from this collection. A happy couple (i.e. young, handsome, healthy, white, heterosexual) stroll on a golf-course by a palm-fringed sea; this is the quality of life for drinkers of Ballantines. Or, to attract the older drinker, a more mature couple are portrayed in fireside domesticity. He mends an antique model ship; she bends over him, showing a good-wifely interest in his hobby.

Martini ('Because you know it's right') pursue the ideal of Young Coupledom with a good-looking pair in skiing gear, and another in tropical outfits, claiming both hemispheres of affluent leisure and excitement.

But it is Remy Martin who trot out every conceivable cliché of the middle-class mating ritual. The couple are mentally summing each other up over dinner — in *his* flat.

Him: 'She's taller I swear it. Can people grow after twenty-five? The tan isn't new either, its an all-year-rounder. I like the haircut. I wonder if she'll notice that I've put on a couple of pounds. I'd forgotten how attractive she is. Those are real pearls too. Where did they come from? I wonder if she still drinks Remy? I hope there's enough.'

Her: 'His flat's changed. Bit of chintz. He looks pretty good, a bit more weight, suits him really. Not sure about the casual look. Where did he learn to cook a soufflé, and who gave him those cufflinks? I wonder what he's thinking about me. Anyway I hope he still drinks Remy.'

We can safely assume that, because they are both chic, tasteful, leisured, attractive and rich, they will end up in bed together, after a few drinks of Remy.

Pairing off with a man is the bait of all these advertisements aimed at women. Strikingly, there are *no* advertisements in this collection which appeal to women on any other basis. Their message conforms to the Norman Mailer stereotype — but only in part. Woman is on earth 'to find the best male possible for herself'. However there is no mention of the second part of her stereotype function — to 'conceive children who will improve the species'. This is reserved for the advertising of other products such as headache tablets and tranquillisers, in which women are portrayed as exhausted, harassed and 'neurotic' housewives and mothers.

In contrast, the majority of advertisements which are aimed at men (still the chief consumers of alcohol), do not take pairing off as their main theme. Symbols of 'the good life' predominate: golf courses, cocktail bars, airport lounges, forests, stags and luscious illustrations of the bottle. They represent the conventionally 'manly' pursuits (sport, hunting); they suggest affluence, virility, or simply the pleasures of drinking.

Stereotyped ideas of men are being used here, just as they are of women, but the implications are entirely different. They suggest that men have a far wider range of interest and greater power in the world than women, and have more to do than simply find a suitable mate.

Harp lager, for instance, promoted their own advertising campaign with this summary of its themes: 'The hero outwits the gorilla, the mean geezer gets his come uppance, the bachelor remains single, and the best man breathes again … It has been described as the most popular consumer campaign for any lager ever.'

Challenge, dominance, competition, remaining unmarried — these are the values which advertisers ascribe to the male.

And when exclusively male sexual imagery is used, as by Strongbow cider, it is in terms, not of alluring lips and nails, but of a hard, sharp arrowhead, in the age-old phallic imagery of aggressive masculinity.

The effects of all these images on our lives as women and women drinkers are many and complex.

On one level, impossible to measure, is the effect on women's self-image and self-esteem. The constant reiteration of the themes that women 'should' be young and beautiful — while at the same time maintaining our primary role as spouse and child rearer — implies that those who don't fit that image and this role are inadequate as women. It also encourages the perception of women as objects, and reinforces sexist assumptions and behaviour. In previous chapters, women have talked about how the resulting negative feelings about themselves can lead into the downward spiral of problem drinking — a devastating illustration of what happens when we internalise images of ourselves, and judge our 'success' or 'failure' in relation to them.

These images also have a negative effect on public attitudes to women's drinking and drunkenness. For as long as the stigma against women's drunkenness persists, women will feel especially guilty about their drinking and will be reluctant to come forward for treatment. The consequences for women's health and well-being are severe.

Furthermore, public attitudes, shaped by these stereotypes, can affect the treatment of women with drink problems so that their chances of recovery are undermined.

In a 'brainstorming exercise' with colleagues in the alcohol field, Shirley Otto came up with this list of adjectives which the participants thought described lay and professional attitudes to male and female alcoholics:

Female alcoholics	Male alcoholics
mad	mad
depressed	sad
ugly	bad
difficult	dirty
demanding	aggressive
wilful	charming
passive	alienated
manipulative	artistic
cunning	unemployed

The adjectives applied to women are without exception negative, and almost all imply moral failure or personality 'defects'. But the words applying to men are less negative — or even positive (i.e. 'charming'), and some of them — 'alienated', 'unemployed' — imply that in the man's case force of circumstances are to blame rather than moral inadequacy.

There is also evidence that women with drink problems are shielded longer than men by their families and GPs, and that women seeking treatment find it more difficult to obtain. And when women are treated for drink problems, they are more likely than men to be treated as *mentally* ill.

The Avon Council on Alcoholism conducted a survey to assess attitudes of workers in the field to treatment and found that 'cultural preconceptions as to appropriate male and female behaviour operate in ways which handicap women. The belief that women's alcoholism is more difficult to detect is matched by a concomitant belief that their alcoholism is somehow more pathological than men's.'[12]

In effect, this means that 'women's chances of receiving psychiatric treatment once their alcohol problem is acknowledged is one in four, whereas men's are only one in six.' And 'women pass through many initial difficulties before they get treatment'. On average, according to the report, women had to wait seven years between the time they first asked for help and the eventual referral for help.

The survey showed that prejudice against women's drunkenness handicaps women in the following ways: 'It was more difficult to identify alcoholism in women ... Women were more reluctant to admit their condition, and ... there was more stigma attached to females as opposed to males.'

Sex-role stereotypes are so pervasive that they, like other deeply-held prejudices, have taken on the weight of common 'truths'. Moral rightness or wrongness is tied up in conformity to widely accepted social norms.

But definitions of male and female in our culture, and of men and women as drinkers, do damage to both. When the image of what we 'should' be does not fit with what we feel ourselves to be, the result is confusion and guilt: 'If a woman does not behave "normally" then questions are asked about her hormones ... or her "poor relations" with her father ... not whether there is something wrong with the identikit picture of the normal woman.'[13]

THE POLITICS OF ALCOHOL

Women are drinking more, and more women are suffering from alcohol related harm as a result.

But this increase must be seen in the context of economic factors — price, income and availability — which encourage us to drink more, and political factors — governmental collusion, parliamentary apathy, huge industrial vested interest, lack of public education — which are doing nothing to stop the increase in drinking.

The question must be asked: why is our society pushing us to seek chemical 'solutions' to our problems? Alcohol *temporarily* lifts depression, reduces anxiety, numbs loneliness and boredom. It helps, temporarily, to make life more bearable — but encourages us to suffer rather than resist.

The answer to the question has to do with the nature of capitalism and the profit priorities of our governments and industrialists.

WOMEN ARE DRINKING MORE

Drinking in Britain is at its highest level for over half a century (following a sharp decline from still higher nineteenth-century levels),[1] and during the 1970s women's rate of consumption roughly doubled.[2] In the twenty years up till 1977, beer drinking in the UK increased by 44 per cent, consumption of wine went up by 265 per cent and our consumption of spirits more than doubled to 119 per cent. Sales of spirits rose 114.5 per cent during the 1970s, with vodka, gin and white rum — women's favourites — showing the biggest increase.[3]

The rate of increase in women's drinking, and the consequent rate of increase in our drinking problems, is growing faster than men's. Health statistics show that more and more women are seeking treatment, becoming ill and dying as a result of drinking. And this rise is in spite of women's traditional reluctance to come forward for help with their drinking problems.

The number of women diagnosed as dependent on alcohol trebled between 1964 and 1975 (while the numbers of men doubled), and deaths from cirrhosis rose by 64 per cent in women between 1970 and 1978 (as compared with 27 per cent in men).[4] The proportion of women to men being treated in mental hospitals for alcoholism has shot up from one quarter of the total two decades ago, to about one half.[5]

DAWN (Drugs, Alcohol, Women — Nationally) say that ten years ago the ratio of females to males seeking and receiving help was one in eight. Now the ratio is at least one in three. Female membership of AA has increased from one in five members in 1972, to one in three in 1981.[6]

More women are getting into trouble with the law over drinking. Although there are still many more male than female drunken offenders (only about eight in a hundred are women), the *rate* of increase in drunken offences is about five times greater amongst women; between 1975 and 1976 female drunken offences rose 14 per cent, as opposed to 3 per cent for men.[7] Women are an even tinier minority in the drunken driving statistics, numbering only one in a hundred offenders when the breath-alyser was first used to test this in 1968. But in the following decade, the rate of convictions for women drunk drivers rose to 3 per cent, while male offences declined.[8]

It is possible that some of these statistics can be explained by factors other than changes in our drinking habits. For instance, the increased numbers of women coming for treatment could be seen as a reflection of a lessening stigma around alcoholism. But, taken together, the evidence of these figures is overwhelming — there is little doubt that there is a real and serious rise in women's drinking.

Not much is known about which groups of women are experiencing more drinking problems, but, according to Mary Bruce of the London Council on Alcoholism, 'women of every age group and social class are coming for counselling and advice'. Similarly, Dr Roger Williams of King's College Hospital Liver Unit says he treats women 'right across the board'.

'Both women in [paid] jobs and women left at home are turning to drink,' according to Derek Rutherford, until recently Director of the National Council on Alcoholism, and 'the latest figures show that of women who come to the local councils for help 50 per cent are housewives and 50 per cent are housewives with [paid] jobs outside the home'.

Almost nothing is known about drinking amongst women from the ethnic minorities, but Black and Chinese people very rarely present themselves for treatment. 'This could be so,' says Shirley Otto, 'because they can't afford to drink, or they just don't come forward, or because their problems, for cultural reasons, are not manifest in alcohol.' In America, fewer Black women than white women do drink, but among those who do there is a higher percentage of heavy drinkers.[9]

And studies in America have found that lesbian women experience a 'much higher rate of alcohol problems than heterosexual women'.[10] Factors contributing to this are isolation, alienation and fear — undoubtedly consequences of society's negative attitude to lesbianism.

Economic reasons for the increase in drinking: People drink more when alcohol is more available to them, both in terms of outlets and of price (see below). And alcohol has become more available to women on both counts.

Alcohol has been getting cheaper while women have been earning more money. The average (median) wage of women trebled in the five years before 1977 (although we still earn only 73 per cent of what men earn), and 'not only have women's average weekly earnings been increasing faster than men's, but the disposable income of women as a group has increased still further because more of them have been coming into employment'.[11] Many of these jobs have been in the service sector and are low paid and/or part-time, but women have gained more control over their expenditure.

At the same time, the real price of alcohol has fallen (in contrast to the real price of food). It has been estimated that in 1950 a manual worker would have had to work twenty-three minutes to earn the price of a pint of beer, and nine minutes for a large loaf of bread. But by 1976 he would only have had to work twelve minutes to earn the pint, and eleven minutes to earn the equivalent loaf.[12] ACCEPT (Alcoholism Community Centres for Educational, Prevention and Treatment) have calculated that between 1967 and 1977 the real price of beer fell by 4 per cent, the real price of wines by 14 per cent, and the real price of spirits by 21 per cent. This means that the drinks most attractive to women — wines and spirits — fell most in real price.

Alcohol has also become easier to buy. During the 1960s the law changed to allow off-licences to open during normal shopping hours, and grocery chains and supermarkets began to open drinks departments. By 1977 half of Britain's supermarkets had licences to sell alcohol and it became 'much easier, more impersonal, and more "respectable" for women to obtain alcohol at a supermarket than it had been in pubs and even in off-licences ... Recent figures have indicated that women have now become more important than men for the bulk of purchases from licenced stores.'[13]

And as women have become more important as consumers, the advertising industry has invested many millions of pounds each year in persuading women to drink more. Some £100 million each year is spent on advertising alcohol, and a large percentage of this goes on advertising drinks which are attractive to women, such as wines and spirits.[14] Even the advertisements for Guinness — traditionally a man's drink and a virility symbol — changed to attract women drinkers.

Advertising has helped make drinking more fashionable for women with its huge campaigns to convince us of the glamour of vermouth and the sophistication of vodka. And for their part, the brewers have invested large sums in the redecoration of pubs, partly to make pubs more attractive to women.[15]

CHEAPER ALCOHOL — MORE DRINKING — MORE ALCOHOLISM

These two areas of change in our drinking — the increase in availability and the increase in alcohol-related problems — are closely linked in a way that has vital implications for the policies and politics of alcohol.

First of all, it's no longer a matter of dispute (except by the brewers and distillers naturally!) that increased availability leads to increased drinking. 'Changes in legislation and in general economic conditions have probably been the major cause of the dramatic increases in consumption that have taken place throughout the world in the past twenty-five years.'[16] And there are plenty of historical examples which show that changes in the law affecting price and availability can alter social attitudes to drinking and our drinking habits — in either direction.

During the sixties, as the developed nations became more prosperous, drinking increased rapidly; it also increased most in those nations whose standard of living showed the greatest rise. This increase coincided with a general drop in the real price of alcohol and a lessening of controls on its sale.

After a late-nineteenth-century high, levels of British drinking sank when licensing and other controls were imposed in 1915 and 1916 — with the aim of boosting the war effort and munitions production.[17] Consumption stayed at this lower level (as did alcohol-related harm such as death from cirrhosis) for as long as alcohol stayed relatively expensive — until the early sixties. Since then, however, we have been returning to the higher, turn-of-the-century levels of drinking (and alcohol related harm), and consumption has virtually doubled in the last quarter century.[18]

The second vital factor in this scenario is that, without doubt, increased consumption in a population leads to an increase in the numbers of people who will suffer from drink problems. This close relationship has been expressed in the 'Ledermann hypothesis', named after the researcher who claimed that if the average consumption of a population is known, the proportion of that population at risk of harm can be calculated from that figure.[19]

And it is widely known that other alcohol related problems rise when consumption rises. Studies in the UK, Canada, the USA and other countries have shown that the rates of death from cirrhosis are so closely linked to the amount consumed in a population that it is possible to work out a country's consumption from its cirrhosis figures.[20]

IMPLICATIONS FOR DEALING WITH ALCOHOL PROBLEMS

These factors have important implications for our definition and treatment of alcohol problems. When alcoholism is considered a 'disease', as it has been in recent years (see chapter 6, part 2), responsibility for treating it and recommending its control becomes the responsibility of the medical profession. But it is now generally accepted that a person develops alcohol dependency as a result of drinking too much for too long, rather than as a result of personality or biochemical factors, and that people do drink more and so develop more problems when alcohol becomes more easily available. Alcohol problems then are, to a large extent, the creation of the alcohol industry, the alcohol lobby and the politicians who regulate the availability of alcohol.

Of course, the medical profession has a large part to play in the treatment of alcohol problems, but, as R.E. Kendell puts it, 'the medical profession and the caring professions in general are just as incapable of dealing effectively with the harm and suffering caused by alcoholism as the medical services of the Armed Forces are incapable of dealing with the harm and suffering caused by war'.[21]

And this is no melodramatic comparison: about five times as many people as the entire population of the Falkland Islands die every year from alcohol in Britain[22] and more than half a million more are estimated to be suffering from alcohol problems.[23] The financial cost of alcohol abuse in England and Wales is estimated to be up to £650 million.[24]

What then, in the face of the huge increases in alcohol problems, are the politicians doing to improve the situation? At present, the answer is — worse than nothing. A series of major reports[25] in recent years have all recommended that the government should control the alcohol supply in the health interest by applying fiscal measures, but instead the rates of alcohol consumption have been allowed to go on rising in the interests of government revenue and drinks trade profits.

A recent Think Tank (Central Policy Review Staff) study[26] reported the huge rise in drinking in recent years and predicted further increases in consumption. It made major recommendations: that tax on drinks should be linked to the retail price index, that there should be more licensing restrictions, tougher drink-driving laws, an investigation into the effects of drink advertising, and a new Advisory Council on Alcohol Policies — none of which have been implemented by the government.

In fact, the government refused to publish the report (which has subsequently been published at Stockholm University), and instead the DHSS produced *Drinking Sensibly,* a booklet which the *British Journal of Addiction* called 'flagrantly misleading' and described as 'halfway between a distasteful joke and an obscene publication ... [Its] essential policy position is that the health of the people is an optional extra'.[27]

Drinking Sensibly does outline the effects, causes and costs of alcohol misuse in this country, all of which should point to the need for action to control price and availability. But when it considers 'Economic Implications' the apparent concern with our toll of disease and death is superseded by a prior consideration — profit: 'A further consideration in setting alcohol duties primarily to serve health and social ends is that this would reduce their value to the government as flexible instruments for *obtaining revenue* [my italics] and for wider economic policy.'[28]

Vested interests: To reduce the damage from alcohol, the country must consume less alcohol, but this reduction would be directly in conflict with the interests of the government, politicians and the drinks trade.

Alcohol is now some 8 per cent of consumer expenditure; for example, in 1979 the British spent about £9,000 million on drink. This massive expenditure brings in about £4,000 million a year in taxes to the government and in 1981 was 6.6 per cent of total government revenue.[29] Britain also has a healthy balance of trade in alcohol; in 1980 our exports were nearly double our imports.[30]

About 750,000 people are directly employed in the drinks industry and this is one of the few categories of employment in this country which is expanding. Employment in the drinks trade grew by about 25 per cent between 1970 and 1980 — a time when employment in other manufacturing industries sank by nearly the same amount.[31]

The drinks industry is powerful and efficient; its large profits have been ploughed back into new production and distribution facilities. The companies that produce alcohol are enormous and have many other interests. The five biggest breweries are among the 126 top companies in the UK.[32] The drinks industry has great political influence and in 1979 it donated at least £107,945 to the Conservative Party and its associates.[33]

Alcohol is also one of the largest sources of revenue to the advertising industry. Some £100 million a year is spent on advertising and promoting alcohol.[34] The media also benefits from the coverage of the many sporting activities sponsored by the drinks industry.

Interests within the government are widespread and conflicting;

sixteen governmental departments have some interest in alcohol.[35] As a result, the government has no coordinated approach to alcohol problems. The Department of Trade obviously wants to maintain the high levels of employment in the industry, while the DHSS should be pulling in the opposite direction. And in that most powerful of government departments, the Treasury, the main concern is that huge revenues from alcohol should not fall.

The apathy of Parliament in acting on alcohol problems is in part explained by the fact that a staggering one in ten MPs has vested interests in alcohol. The alcohol lobby in the Houses of Parliament 'is larger and better supported even than the tobacco lobby', writes Mike Daube in the *Times Health Supplement*. 'The disturbing difference is that the alcohol lobby has not yet been wheeled into action: there is no need — its ascendency in Parliament is broadly accepted, and has scarcely been challenged.'[36]

In 1981, thirty-four MPs had a 'direct financial interest' in the drinks industry (i.e. those MPs with a 'clear financial link with the drinks industry or with a major advertising or PR agency with substantial alcohol accounts, or [with] ownership of pubs or hotels').[37]

A further thirty-nine MPs had an 'indirect interest' in alcohol (i.e. 'links through advertising, PR, newspapers' or other business connections).[38]

And before becoming Ministers — when MPs are obliged to give up their directorships and consultancies — eleven Tory MPs held direct interests in alcohol.[39] Geoffrey Finsberg, now a junior Minister at the DHSS, was previously the parliamentary adviser to the National Union of Licensed Victuallers. Norman Fowler, Secretary of State at the DHSS, was director of a subsidiary of J. Walter Thompson, one of the biggest advertising agencies in the world, with large alcohol accounts.[40]

'Fiscal legislation apart, alcohol sale and promotion is relatively free of constraints,' writes Mike Daube:

> There are few serious limitations on industry and promotion, no health warnings, easy access — with ever more outlets such as supermarkets, and all but ignored legislation on sales to minors. Governments of either complexion have been recommended firmer measures by their own advisors, but still there is little action. Even education — the last resort of the politician who wants to avoid legislation — is so low-key and ill-funded as to be almost unbelievable.[41]

And politicians have a major interest (apart from their own heavy drinking habits) in avoiding legislation: the electorate doesn't want it. A *Sunday Times* MORI poll showed in 1980 that the public is strongly opposed to large increases in the price of alcohol (74 per cent), and to a ban on advertising alcohol (70 per cent). There is also strong opposition to banning supermarket sales (63 per cent) and to tougher laws (50 per cent).

The Opposition: Meanwhile, the anti-alcohol lobby remains weak and badly organised. The four main alcohol charities are the National Council on Alcoholism (NCA), the Medical Council on Alcoholism (MCA), the Alcohol Education Centre (AEC), and the Federation of Alcoholic Rehabilitation Establishments (FARE). All of these were criticised in a 1982 DHSS/NCVO (National Council for Voluntary Organisations) report,[42] which looked at their effectiveness in reducing alcohol damage and found 'serious deficiencies'.

The MCA was criticised for having little success in helping GPs, and for failing to break resistance from medical schools to get alcoholism included in the curriculum. The AEC was criticised for running impractical and underused courses in alcohol education, and FARE was found wanting in the focus of its aims and objectives. The NCA, said the report, had failed to provide a national focus for publishing the problems of alcohol misuse, although it had done useful work in industry.

The only one of these organisations to have taken any serious initiative over women's drinking is FARE, which has links (through its women workers) with DAWN. When I asked Derek Rutherford, then Director of the NCA, if the NCA thought women had separate problems with alcohol, he at first said, 'No comment' — and then referred me to a female colleague: 'I would prefer you to have a woman's views,' he said, 'instead of [views] from us MCPs.'

When I asked him why there had not been a huge campaign from the NCA to alert women to the dangers of drinking in pregnancy, he reluctantly replied, 'Because of the power of vested interests. It is time [a campaign] does happen here as it has happened in the USA. This is all I dare say at this stage.'

Since the critical report was published, it has seemed likely that the alcohol charities will lose their government grants and be replaced with a new umbrella organisation.

In the meantime, our drinking, and our casualties from drinking, are likely to increase. The drinks industry at least, is counting on it: 'it is the firm view of the industry that consumption will continue to increase ... and a number of interests in the wine trade both in this country and overseas have independently assessed the UK as a market with great potential for growth.'[43] Women are also expected to misuse alcohol more as incomes continue to grow, and the inhibitions on drinking amongst women relax.[44] This is a particularly cruel function of 'market forces', especially in view of women's special vulnerability to alcohol-related harm and the effects on the foetus(see chapter 8), and in the absence of education to warn us about this.

The last ten years have seen an 'alcoholism epidemic [which is] a public health disaster of historic proportions', according to the *British Journal of Addiction*.[45] To combat this disaster we need educational, legislative and political changes.

We need a major series of educational campaigns on the problems of alcohol, especially on the health risks to women and the dangers of drinking during pregnancy. We need regular tax increases to maintain the price of alcohol relative to the cost of living; we need a ban on alcohol advertising, a reduction in outlets, stiffer laws on drunken driving and a ban on the loosening of licensing laws.

We need better care for women with alcohol problems, and above all we need to change the social conditions which drive women to seek chemical 'solutions' to their problems and which contribute to women's lack of confidence and low self-esteem.

It will be no easy task against the massed vested interests of industry, Parliament, and a government which 'is willing to trade the nation's health for profit and expedience'.[46]

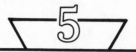

BAD NEWS FOR WOMEN DRINKERS

Alcohol affects women differently from men and its ill effects are more severe in women:

— Our bodies are generally smaller and have a higher proportion of fat to water, which means that alcohol is more concentrated in our body fluids.

— We are more prone to liver damage and to other alcohol-related diseases than are men. We are more liable to develop digestive and nutritional problems as a consequence of drinking, and we are more likely to become dependent on alcohol.[1]

— Our response to alcohol can change during ovulation and menstruation, and we risk damage to the foetus if we drink during pregnancy.

— Millions of women in the UK are prescribed tranquillising drugs which, in combination with alcohol, make us more vulnerable to physical and psychological damage.

Researchers are now saying that women should limit themselves to less than four units of alcohol a day. (One unit is equivalent to half a pint of beer, a single English measure of spirits or a four fluid ounce glass of wine.)[1]

This is depressing news to those of us who enjoy a 'good drink', and as with all depressing news, the temptation is to forget it. It is also unwelcome for its potential as cheap-shot ammunition for arguments that we are 'weaker vessels', that women 'can't hold their drink' and so on. But to ignore the evidence of these differences is no favour to women either. It has too long been a tradition in the alcohol field that sex-related differences don't matter, and *this* is the sexist assumption. 'Until recently, female alcoholism was not regarded as legitimate grounds for professional concern,' say the Avon Council on Alcoholism, and 'between 1929 and 1970 the topic stimulated only twenty-nine studies in the English language'.[2]

Although the library shelves are groaning with learned tomes about alcohol, most of the books refer to 'alcoholics' without mentioning the sex of the subject. It is assumed that 'alcoholics' are men, and there is a great shortage of accurate information about the effects of alcohol on women.

'It is a strange fact,' said the *British Journal on Alcohol and Alcoholism* in 1982, 'that although women constitute at least half of the population, most of the information that we have about alcoholism is related to men and male rodents.'[3]

In the course of my research I found only one British book and a handful of pamphlets and articles which were specifically about the effects of alcohol on women.[4] Almost every other publication referred to the drinker as 'he', apart from occasional references to women as exceptions from the rule. So, inevitably, much of the information in this chapter is based on research done on men and although I have tried to fill those gaps which I became aware of and have adapted information where possible, there could be more ways not yet known to us in which alcohol affects women.

Where discoveries have been made about alcohol's effects on women — as there were in the nineteenth century and in the early 1970s about alcohol-related birth defects — these have been largely ignored, or even suppressed (see chapter 9).

There is no longer any doubt that drink can damage the foetus, but to date no British government has made this a public health issue. While American government officials have launched a campaign to warn women to avoid alcohol entirely during pregnancy, the British medical establishment is still fudging the issue.

As late as 1979 the Royal College of Psychiatrists was still saying that 'heavy drinking' — i.e. 'a couple of bottles of wine taken each day is getting into the danger area' for pregnant women. This was a ridiculous statement in view of the fact that one bottle of wine a day would be a health risk to many women, pregnant or not.

Fortunately, the College has revised its statement and now advises pregnant women *not to drink at all*. But as yet few British women are informed of the risks, while clinics and surgeries remain bare of the posters and leaflets which could prevent more tragedies.

And in treatment as much as in prevention women would stand to gain a great deal from the recognition that we have separate problems and need separate attention. Despite the increases in women's alcohol problems, the services that do exist for women have been described as 'wholly inadequate'.[5]

BLAMING WOMEN

Researchers are now beginning to turn their attention to *women* and alcohol. But that is not necessarily a good thing in itself. What does matter is the *form* which this attention takes, annd the ways in which new information is made public.

Some women are concerned that the interest of the male-dominated medical profession in women's alcohol problems is being expressed in unacceptable ways. Already it seems that some researchers are more interested in treating the 'interesting' female organs than in looking at *why* a woman should be putting her health at risk through drinking. The female liver becomes more important than its owner; the female's capacity to give birth deserves more care than the potential mother. After long neglect of women, research money is at last being made available — but for the study of alcohol's effect on *women as child bearers*.

There is also the danger that the cause of alcohol abuse could become a fashionable stick for beating women, blaming them for the neglect of their families, and for the handicap of their babies. Such implications at once burden women with guilt for sometimes irreversible tragedies, perpetuate the stereotype of women as irresponsible creatures (see chapter 3), and reinforce the traditional roles of women as wives and mothers with chief responsibility to the family.

A professed concern for mothers' and babies' welfare — as expressed by Right to Life campaigners (anti-abortionists) — can disguise a fundamental attack on women. The issue of the 'unborn child' is highly charged, both morally and politically, and women who have claimed the right to control their own fertility in campaigns for contraception and abortion have had bitter experience of the manipulative tactics used to oppose this demand.

Typically, emotive appeals are made in the name of the foetus, which instil guilt in women, suggest that we are unnatural and criminal if we choose not to give birth, and, by implication, reduce women to the function of 'breeders'.

We need to be on our guard against such assumptions creeping into publicity about alcohol-related birth defects. If women are going to be informed, it must not be in a tone which reflects traditional horror at the 'bad mother' (see chapter 3) and that suggests we are irresponsible and in need of constraint — if only in the interests of future generations.

And for as long as individual women are held to blame for being 'bad mothers' and/or problem drinkers, attention is diverted from the social and psychological reasons behind women's alcohol abuse. Meanwhile the profiteering of industry and government in allowing the rates of drink consumption to rise so high is forgotten, and successive governments' failures to warn women through health campaigns are ignored.

INFORMATION — OR EXPLOITATION?

Where there has been debate about publicising the issue of alcohol-related birth defects, it has been very heated. On the one hand, it is clearly important that women should be told of the risks. On the other hand, such information has to be handled with great care. Those doctors who have heard about the dangers have to consider whether anxiety and guilt in an already pregnant woman who has been drinking might be more harmful than the unquantifiable risks of alcohol.

And some feminists fear that the risks to pregnant women could too easily be exploited and sensationalised in the press. A far greater stigma is still attached to women with drink problems than to men, and the kind of publicity that reinforces this sense of shame only drives women into the vicious circle of guilty and secret drinking. Such women are even less likely to seek help before their drinking has damaged their (especially vulnerable) health.

In the course of the debate, accusations and recriminations have been hurled between researchers, campaigners and government officials. Some of those who want to publicise the issue have been called alarmists, frauds[6] or cranks by the opposition. Those who don't have been accused of everything from indifference to 'mafia' style intimidation and concealment of the facts.[7]

But information — that the causes and results of drinking in women are different from those in men — is vital if we are to make choices about our own health. At the moment, much of the existing information, and the power to make and publicise new discoveries, is in the hands of a few, mostly male, individuals. Yet as Fiona Richmond of DAWN puts it, 'the only people who really care about women are women. And women aren't represented in the research field. If we want accurate information we have to get in there and get it ourselves.'

The aim of the following chapters is to provide some of that information (which is likely to be incomplete because of the dearth of research into women and alcohol). Women should have early access to knowledge which could mean the difference between health and avoidable ill health — for ourselves and for our children. The manner in which we are informed is crucial, but informed we must be.

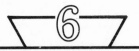

ABOUT ALCOHOL

WHAT IS ALCOHOL?

> Alcohol, like fire, was bound to exist. The mere storage of many
> products of the earth could result, under certain circumstances, in
> the formation of an alcoholic beverage. Alcohol, like fire, is the
> source of both good and evil. It can serve society meaningfully as a
> ritual symbol, as a means of enhancing food, as a tension releaser,
> as a way of developing social ease. Yet man [sic] has, under its
> influence, committed crimes of all sorts and at all levels. Alcohol,
> like fire, symbolises the paradox of the human condition.[1]

Alcohol has many meanings: chemically, *alcohols* are a family of substances, but the one which we drink is C_2H_5OH, or ethyl alcohol, a colour-
less liquid with a sharp, burning taste. It is produced when yeast ferments
the sugars in the raw materials of the drink. These sugars occur naturally
in fruits and cereals such as barley, grapes and apples.

The alcohol concentration of a fermented brew can be increased
tremendously when it is boiled and the vapour is collected, cooled and
reliquefied. It is this process, distillation, which produces the spirits we
drink.

Medically, alcohol is a depressant drug that slows the activity of the
brain. Far back in history its medicinal qualities were highly valued and it
was called 'the elixir of life' and reputed to have great powers of healing.
It has also been used as a pain reliever (about as efficient as aspirin), and
as a surgical anaesthetic (not efficient).

Alcohol is also a kind of food, containing as many calories as fat (seven
per gram). It is also a disinhibiting, consciousness-altering drug,
accepted in most societies as a legal, social psychotropic for adult use. In
large enough quantities it is a lethal poison.

But most commonly alcohol means 'booze' — and specifically the
intoxicating ingredient in alcoholic beverages. There are various ways of
expressing the amount of this ingredient, but the most useful is the standard unit system. One unit of an alcoholic drink is the amount of that
drink which contains approximately half an ounce of absolute alcohol.

This is the amount that the liver can dispose of (oxidise) per hour in 'an average eleven-stone person'.[2] (Assuming that the 'average person' means a man, a unit of alcohol will have a greater effect on most women.) In other words, it takes about one hour to sober up for each unit of alcohol consumed.

One unit of alcohol is found in approximately half a pint of beer, a single English pub measure of spirits (⅙ gill), a glass of wine (4 fluid ounces), or a small glass (½ oz) of fortified wine (i.e. port or sherry).[3]

Another way to express the amount of intoxicating ingredient in drink is to describe the percentage of the liquid which is pure or absolute alcohol. Spirits contain approximately 40 per cent, fortified wine contains about 20 per cent, table wine about 10 per cent and beer about 5 per cent of absolute alcohol.

This system (called the European, or Gay-Lussac system) of measuring alcoholic strength, can be confused with the British 'proof spirit' system. Our system dates back to an archaic method of measuring or 'proving' the concentration of alcohol in water by adding gun powder to the mixture. If the mixture ignited this meant that it was not less than half alcohol. Modern proof spirit is a mixture of 57 per cent spirit and 43 per cent water, so that if a spirit is described as 100 per cent proof, it contains 100 per cent of the spirit/water mixture. A bottle of gin marked 70° proof should be 70 per cent of the proof strength spirit. This is equivalent to 40 per cent (European) absolute alcohol.[4]

WHAT HAPPENS WHEN YOU DRINK?

Alcohol is generally swallowed and absorbed into the blood from the stomach and small intestine — although its intoxicating fumes can also be inhaled into the lungs in quite large quantities. It can also be absorbed very fast through the rectum.

The rate at which you absorb alcohol depends on several factors. If you drink on an empty stomach it will be absorbed quickly. This is why one drink before a meal often feels much more powerful than two or three afterwards. Food, especially fatty food, in the stomach will slow down the absorption process so that the alcohol concentration in the blood of a person who has just eaten will be about a quarter of the level reached in someone who has been fasting.

Bubbly drinks, such as champagne, sparkling wines, and spirits combined with a fizzy mixer will also make you drunk faster. This is because the action of the bubbles stimulates the valve which separates stomach and small intestine so that it opens wide and the alcohol passes through rapidly.

This same valve, the pylorus, will shut tightly and go into spasm if you drink too much too fast. This makes you feel sick and vomiting often follows. It is a mechanism which protects the body against larger amounts of alcohol than it can cope with.

From the gut, alcohol is absorbed into the blood and within minutes spreads throughout the body, reaching even the bones. In pregnant women, it passes into the blood of the foetus and, in women who are breast feeding, it passes into the milk.

The blood circulation then takes it to the lungs, heart and liver. Some of it is excreted from the lungs, giving your breath the smell of alcohol. Some of it is also eliminated through the kidneys and skin (which can also smell of alcohol), but the liver does about 90 per cent of the work of elimination.

If you drink at the rate of about one unit per hour, alcohol will not accumulate, but drinking faster than this or gulping drinks will end in intoxication. Whether or not you feel 'drunk' as a result will depend on the way your body 'handles' alcohol in the intricate process of absorption, distribution and elimination, and on your level of tolerance and general state of being.

And contrary to popular belief you cannot hurry the sobering-up process with black coffee, cold showers or fresh air. None of these will have any effect on the concentration of alcohol in your blood; they will only make you feel more awake. Sobering up is simply a matter of time.

WHAT DOES ALCOHOL DO TO YOU?

Most people are surprised to hear that alcohol is technically a 'depressant' as it has the effect of making them feel, initially at least, the opposite of depressed. But this 'lifting' effect is the result of the depressant or anaesthetising action of alcohol on the higher centres of the brain, home of the super-ego. This is the part of the brain which controls our self-critical faculties, and when it is depressed, anxiety, caution and self-consciousness are reduced. Initially, this leaves the way clear for the feelings of confidence, relaxation, and euphoria which are the goals of most drinkers.

Women and men react differently at different times to alcohol. You might have four pints one night and feel as happy as a lark — and two weeks later find yourself getting sick or in tears after drinking the same amount. But these are, in general terms, the stages of intoxication:

The first stage is 'happy'. You feel talkative, sociable and relaxed. You have fewer inhibitions and worries. There is some loss of judgement and efficiency.

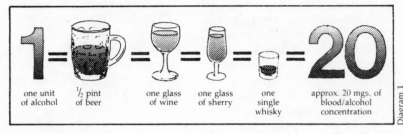

one unit of alcohol | ½ pint of beer | one glass of wine | one glass of sherry | one single whisky | approx. 20 mgs. of blood/alcohol concentration

Diagram 1

1 bottle of spirits | 1 bottle of fortified wine | 1 bottle of table wine | 1 pint of beer

Diagram 2

What are the various kinds of alcoholic drink?

The second stage is 'excited'. Your behaviour is emotional and erratic, your thinking is impaired and your reactions slowed. Your judgement is poor and you lose control over some of your actions.

The third stage is 'confused'. You are staggering. You feel disoriented, moody, fearful, angry. Speech is slurred and you are seeing double.

The fourth stage is 'in a stupor'. You can't stand or walk. You are barely conscious, apathetic and inert. You are probably vomiting and incontinent.

The fifth stage is 'in a coma' and you are completely unconscious with few or no reflexes. This state may end in death from respiratory paralysis.[5]

HOW MUCH ALCOHOL?

How many drinks will take you to which stage of intoxication? Most regular drinkers can answer this question for themselves — and will know that their friends will give different answers depending on a number of factors.

For medical and legal purposes Blood Alcohol Concentration (BAC), or the number of milligrams of alcohol per millilitre of blood, is used to find out how much a person has consumed. It is important to stress however, both that these figures can vary enormously due to a number of factors, and that alcohol is likely to have a greater effect upon women. One estimate by the Office of Health Economics (OHE) is that a pint of beer or its equivalent will give a BAC of 30 after about one hour. In an 'average person' (we can assume they mean a man) this BAC should produce a 'sense of mild well-being'. Four units of alcohol (see diagram 1) will produce a BAC of about 60 which may result in 'loss of muscular control and abnormal eye movements'.[2] Yet this is still below the British drinking and driving legal limit of 80 milligrams.

From BACs of 90 to 100 the drinker generally suffers marked impairment. From 200 to 300 most people will be semi-conscious or unconscious, and at 500 or over the drinker could well die.[6] One more practical way of remembering roughly what booze does to you is the 'Four Ds':

100mg — dizzy and delightful   200mg — drunk and disorderly
300mg — dead drunk   400mg — danger of death

Workers with blood levels between 30mg and 100mg have 'considerably more accidents' than those with below 30mg, according to the Health Education Council. And car drivers, they say, are more likely to have an accident after even a pint of beer (30mg). At 80mg the risk of accident is four times greater and after about five pints (150mg) the risk is twenty-five times higher.[7]

But the snag is — and many drivers complain about it — that we have no simple way of predicting how drunk one person will get after how much drink. Regular drinkers are inclined to scoff at these estimates of how much booze makes them incapable as bearing no relation to how they feel after four pints on a Friday evening. And it is true that 'rates' of getting drunk and sobering up can only be estimates as individuals and their levels of tolerance vary so greatly. And again, most of the work on assessing these rates refer to the drinker as 'he'.

How much drink you can 'hold' depends on how much you are used to. It is also affected by your state of mind and general health, and by how much food you have eaten and how recently. Your body weight and stage of menstrual cycle will also make for differences.

And, as I've said, alcohol *does* affect men and women differently. Very little alcohol enters fatty tissue as this tissue has a poor blood supply, and women have a higher proportion of fat to water than men. Young women have about 50 per cent of their total body weight in the form of water, as opposed to 60 per cent for young men. This means that even if a woman is the same weight as a man, she is going to get drunk faster as the pool of liquid in which her drink is diffused is smaller — and so the concentration of alcohol will be higher. And most women are smaller than men to start with, so that alcohol's effects are even more concentrated.

 TOLERANCE

Perhaps the most important factor to affect how 'drunk' you get is your level of tolerance to alcohol. Most of us can remember getting giggly or silly or weepy on just a couple of drinks when we first took alcohol, and many beginner drinkers get sick and giddy as well.

But although this response shows itself in physical discomforts, it is actually the brain's reaction to a rush of unfamiliar sensations. People who smoke marijuana for the first time often feel sick for the same reasons, in reaction to the alteration in their consciousness.

After more experience with drink (as with drugs) most people are better able to cope with it, and in larger quantities. This change shows that they are developing psychological or behavioural tolerance to drink. Some heavy drinkers eventually 'learn' to cope with huge amounts of alcohol without seeming to be drunk — a dangerous situation for their health. It also happens that after a high degree of tolerance has been maintained for years in heavy drinkers the process may go into reverse, and she or he starts getting drunk very quickly on small amounts.

This process of developing tolerance has been compared to that of a child ('he' again ...) growing up.

> Just as a newborn baby, unable at first to coordinate any of his movements, learns eventually to grasp with his hands, then stand up, then walk, and talk, then operate computers or space vehicles, so the drunk, given sufficient experience, can learn to cope with his state. In his vaudeville days for instance, W.C. Fields was able to perform six acts daily of intricate jugglery while on a one-to-two-quarts-of-gin-per-day drinking regime. Fields had 'learned' the drunken state and could function within it.[8]

In addition to this behavioural tolerance which most 'social' drinkers soon develop, the body has the capacity to develop a higher level of physical tolerance to alcohol. Very heavy drinkers can 'learn' to metabolise alcohol more quickly than usual, and surgeons have found that alcoholic patients require larger doses of anaesthetics than non-drinkers. This is because, together with physical tolerance to alcohol, very heavy drinkers may show a cross-resistance to substances like ether and chloroform.[9]

On one level, then, learning how to handle drink is valued as a social skill which stops most of us making fools of ourselves in pubs or at parties. But on another level developing tolerance is a dangerously insidious process, which allows us to pass for sober when we are not. It is a process which is linked to the so-called 'alcohol-dependence syndrome' or 'alcoholism' (see chapter 10) in which many drinkers get well out of their depth — before they realise the danger.

TIMING

The timing of your drinking will also affect how drunk you feel — and how you feel when drunk — independently of blood alcohol levels.

By eleven o'clock at night, after a few pleasant pints in the pub, you will most likely be in a mellow mood, confident and relaxed. Your blood alcohol level is probably about 80mg. You are on the 'up-curve' of drinking and enjoying the (subjectively) stimulating effects of alcohol.

But although drink makes you *feel* more capable by removing your anxieties, it actually stops you from functioning as well as you do when sober — unless you are an exceptionally nervous character. Alcohol has a negative effect on concentration, memory, judgement and insight, and limits your attention span and reaction time — all good reasons not to drive at this level of drinking.

Not all of the parts of your brain are affected to the same extent, or the same amounts of drink which make you 'drunk' would at the same time affect systems like your breathing mechanism. It is the most sophisticated processes of thought and coordination which are clouded at first, so that your movements become clumsy and your thinking erratic.

Had you left the pub in this mellow state at eleven o'clock and gone to a party where you had more drinks, your confidence might have grown into euphoria. You would have felt able for anything, capable of saying anything to anyone. This is the drinking 'up-curve'.

Yet the next morning, while going through the painful process of sobering up, your blood alcohol level would again pass the 80mg point — on the way down. In contrast to the same point the night before when your level was 80mg, you are likely to feel clumsy, inept and probably anxious and guilty. You are on the drinking 'down-curve' and you are feeling the depressant and toxic effects of alcohol.

Drinkers do commonly judge themselves to be less inept while getting drunk than when hungover, but tests on memory, attention and co-ordination have shown that the reverse is true. Both men and women score *less* in these categories on the up-curve than they do on the down-curve, but, on the up-curve women score less than men in motor co-ordination, and more than men on attention. Driving requires both of these skills — which means that one sex is no safer than the other in taking the car home from the party.

And on the morning after — or any morning — you are unlikely to want a stiff drink as soon as you wake up (unless you have problems of dependence and withdrawal). By the evening, however, 'when the sun is over the yard-arm' — a pint of beer is a much more tempting prospect.

It has been suggested that we have some sort of biological clock which dictates the timing of healthy drinking habits — from which follow pub opening hours and social conventions about when you should drink. In a rather objectionable experiment with mice, 60 per cent of the animals reportedly died when dosed with vodka at their time of awakening, while the same dose given to the mice as a 'nightcap' killed 12 per cent of them.

One somewhat romantic conclusion is that 'the person who waits until sundown to start drinking is more in tune with the tides of life than the one who starts first thing in the morning'.[10] Whether this is true or not, the person who waits until sundown is certainly less likely to develop alcohol problems.

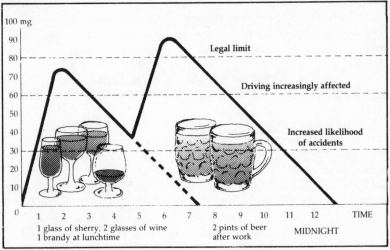

What happens if you have been drinking at lunchtime and then drink again in the late afternoon?

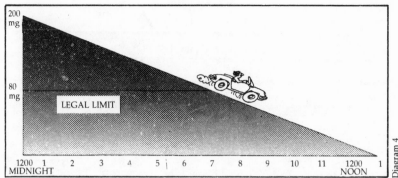

200 mg

80 mg

LEGAL LIMIT

1200 1 2 3 4 5 6 7 8 9 10 11 1200 1
MIDNIGHT NOON

Diagram 4

Drinking twice a day: Because your system can only metabolise so much alcohol in a given time, drinking twice a day or topping up throughout the day will have a cumulative effect.

Men, more than women, are in (better) paid jobs and follow a pattern of going to the pub at lunch hour and again after work. The following explanation, based on a Health Education Council leaflet, assumes this male pattern (its illustrations show men), but it does apply with equal or greater force to women who drink twice a day.

If you have a boozy lunch which includes, say, a sherry, two glasses of wine and a liqueur, and then pop down to the pub when it opens after work for a couple of pints of lager, you are likely to get a lot drunker than you bargained for.

The lunchtime drink would raise your blood alcohol level to about 85mg. This will sink gradually throughout the afternoon, but at 5.30 p.m. will still be above the sober level. After two evening pints, however, your blood alcohol level will be back above the legal driving limit — at about 90mg. Not only can you lose your licence at this stage but you are four times more likely to have an accident than when sober (see diagram 3).

The same banking-up effect can affect your morning-after. If you were to go to bed at one a.m. after four glasses of wine and a double brandy — or six pints of beer — your blood alcohol level would be about 200mg.

The alcohol in your blood would still be above the legal driving limit at 8.00 a.m., and you would be more likely to have an accident at work until mid-morning (see diagram 4).

THE MENSTRUAL CYCLE

Your reaction to alcohol is also likely to vary according to the stages of your menstrual cycle. Many women find that just a couple of drinks — which might ordinarily have a mildly mellowing effect — will make them feel quite unexpectedly drunk while they are ovulating or premenstrual. (It is worth bearing this in mind if you are driving.)

It could be that alcohol is absorbed more fully and quickly and with increased effect when women are premenstrual. Our tissues at this time are more ready to retain water and so may retain more alcohol in that water.

As a result of these fluctuations, women have a less predictable response to drink than men do. Women on the Pill will have a more regular response, but they will metabolise alcohol more slowly and so stay drunk longer.

And many women drink for relief from premenstrual tension, post-natal depression, and from depression around the time of menopause. Alcohol with its cheering, relaxing effect, *seems* like the ideal balm for these problems. But for some women, the long-term consequences of the 'cheering drink' can be severe.

Judy Lever, in her book on premenstrual tension, writes that 'since alcohol in the long term is a depressant, anxiety-producing, addictive drug, you may find over-drinking becoming a regular monthly routine, and the slide into alcoholism begins'.[1]

It is common for women to drink more before their periods in the hopes of curing the premenstrual 'blues'. In an American survey, 67 per cent of women alcoholics related their drinking bouts to their menstrual cycle and all of them said that their drinking had begun or increased during the premenstrual period.[2]

Alcohol clinics like ACCEPT in London have also found that women drink more heavily in the week before their period and are inclined to relapse — if they have been trying to stay 'dry' — in this week. Charles Vetter of ACCEPT identifies the 'vulnerability period' as ten days or so before menstruation. He says that during this time the extra strain of PMT can sap women's will-power and make them feel miserable. A likely response is for a woman to start drinking again to cheer herself up.

Vetter has asked women to keep a diary of their drinking habits and periods and has consistently found that women who have been coping well, will start to feel desperate before their period and will turn to alcohol. One of ACCEPT's women clients had seven relapses into drinking — and her diary showed that all of them coincided with the three and four days before her period.

THE DIGESTIVE SYSTEM: EAT, DRINK AND BE MERRY

As far as your digestive system is concerned, alcohol — like much else that we swallow — is beneficial in moderation and damaging in excess. This is not the place for a gourmet guide to drink: suffice to say that alcohol can be a delicious accompaniment to food as an aperitif, an ingredient, and as a complement to a meal. And it can be delicious in itself.

But as a type of food, alcohol's value is very limited. It gives as many calories as fat (seven Calories per gram) and alcoholics are said to literally 'run on spirit'.

These are 'empty' calories however, with none of the minerals, proteins or vitamins which are essential to nutrition. Whenever alcohol is substituted for food — as it often is in 'liquid lunches' or 'binges' — the body is deprived of essential nutrients.

Alcohol also interferes with the body's ability to use other sources of energy. Alcoholics often neglect to eat and it has been said that alcoholism is the major cause of malnutrition in the western world.

And all drinkers know that alcohol makes you urinate a lot. This is not simply a result of taking in all that extra liquid; it happens because one of the hormones which controls the amount of urine your body produces is affected by drink. When you have alcohol in your body, too little of this hormone is produced, and so too much urine results.

GETTING FAT

Drinking can make you fat — unless you balance your intake of food and alcohol properly, and take exercise. The number of calories that your body burns depends on various factors such as your metabolism, your size and how physically active you are. But very roughly women need about 2,000 Calories a day to stay at the same weight (as opposed to 2,500 to 3,000 for men).

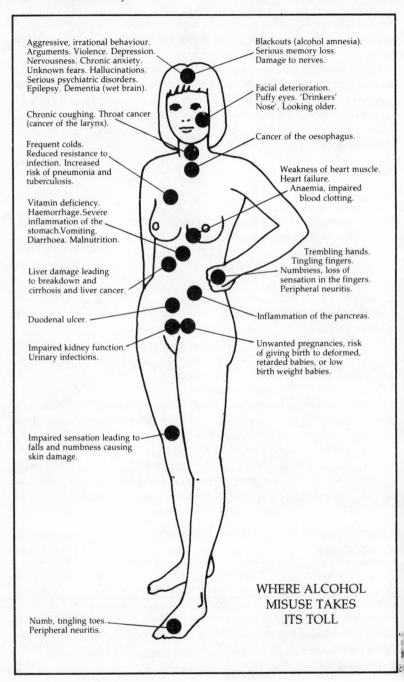

Aggressive, irrational behaviour. Arguments. Violence. Depression. Nervousness. Chronic anxiety. Unknown fears. Hallucinations. Serious psychiatric disorders. Epilepsy. Dementia (wet brain).

Chronic coughing. Throat cancer (cancer of the larynx).

Frequent colds. Reduced resistance to infection. Increased risk of pneumonia and tuberculosis.

Vitamin deficiency. Haemorrhage. Severe inflammation of the stomach. Vomiting. Diarrhoea. Malnutrition.

Liver damage leading to breakdown and cirrhosis and liver cancer.

Duodenal ulcer.

Impaired kidney function. Urinary infections.

Impaired sensation leading to falls and numbness causing skin damage.

Numb, tingling toes. Peripheral neuritis.

Blackouts (alcohol amnesia). Serious memory loss. Damage to nerves.

Facial deterioration. Puffy eyes. 'Drinkers' Nose'. Looking older.

Cancer of the oesophagus.

Weakness of heart muscle. Heart failure. Anaemia, impaired blood clotting.

Trembling hands. Tingling fingers. Numbness, loss of sensation in the fingers. Peripheral neuritis.

Inflammation of the pancreas.

Unwanted pregnancies, risk of giving birth to deformed, retarded babies, or low birth weight babies.

WHERE ALCOHOL
MISUSE TAKES
ITS TOLL

Alcohol is full of calories. A pint of beer has about 180 Calories, a pub measure of whisky has about 50 and a glass of wine has about 80-100 (see diagram 5).

This means that by drinking five pints of beer in the course of a day, you are taking in about *half* of your daily calorie requirement. If you continue eating normally (i.e. at 2,000 Calories a day), which you need to do to maintain the level of essential nutrients present in food but not in alcohol, you will probably gain weight. It has been estimated that alcoholic beverages now account for approximately one-twentieth of the nation's calorie intake.

It takes about 3,000 Calories to add a pound of fat to the body, so if you continue eating normally and drinking five pints a day you could put on about a pound a week.

The best way to cope with these extra calories is simply to drink less. But if you won't or can't do that, extra exercise will help to burn them up.

Taking alcohol before and with meals has long been considered a 'civilised' custom in many cultures — and with good reason. Apart from the social and psychological advantages of having a drink at mealtimes, there is a physical bonus in that moderate amounts of drink aid digestion, hence the practice of taking an aperitif and of drinking wine with meals. A few drinks stimulates the flow of saliva and gastric acid in the stomach. These juices are necessary for digestion, but people with peptic ulcers should avoid alcohol as the extra acidity causes discomfort.

And too much alcohol has an adverse effect, delaying the absorption of food and causing vomiting. High concentrations of alcohol will also irritate the stomach lining, causing inflammation and erosions. About a third of heavy drinkers have chronic stomach problems, such as gastritis. The duodenum (beginning of the small intestine) and the oesophagus (tube leading from the mouth to the stomach) are also badly affected by too much drink. Women drinkers are especially prone to stomach and duodenal ulcers, nutritional problems and anaemia. Cancer of the oesophagus is also more common in alcoholics than in the rest of the population, and heavy smoking has a 'synergic' (working together) effect, multiplying the risk of cancer already increased by drinking.[3]

YOUR LIVER

The liver has many intricate and important functions. It is the largest gland in the body. It fuels us (by maintaining our level of blood sugar, the only form of energy the brain can use). It purifies our blood (by removing toxins and impurities). It breaks down proteins and stores fats and vitamins. It also handles the chemical breakdown of alcohol — and in the

Calories in alcoholic drinks:

Beers: per pint		
Bitter		180
Brown ale		170
Stout		200
Light Ale		150
Mild Ale		150
Pale Ale		180
Most home brewed beers		240
Pils (per bottle)		105

Ciders: per half pint		
Dry		100
Sweet		120
Babycham		78

Lagers: per pint		160-180
Stella Artois		240
Special strength lager (half pint bottle)		205
Non-alcoholic lager (275 ml can)		45-55

Sherry: (⅓ gill)		
Dry		55
Medium		60
Cream		65

Port: (⅓ gill)		75

Spirits: (pub measure: ⅙ gill)		
Brandy		75
Whisky		58
Rum		75
Gin		55
Vodka		63

Wines: (per glass)		
Dry white		75
Sweet white		100
Rosé		80
Dry red		80
Sweet red		95
Champagne		90-110
Non-alcoholic wine		30

Aperitifs: (pub measure: ⅓ gill)		
Martini, Dry		84
Martini, Sweet		98
Ouzo		60
Pernod		65
Campari		111

Liqueurs: (pub measure: ⅙ gill)		
Benedictine		90
Cointreau or Drambuie		85
Creme de Menthe		80
Grand Marnier		80
Baileys Irish Cream		85

Mixers:		
Fruit juices (bottles)		
Grapefruit		65
Orange		60
Tomato		25
Soda water or mineral water		0
Bitter lemon (4 fl oz)		40
Tonic water (4 fl oz)		25-40
Lime juice cordial (1 fl oz)		25
Dry Ginger Ale (4 fl oz)		15
Lemonade (4 fl oz)		30
Cola		80

process, because of differences in our metabolism and immune systems, women are far more vulnerable to damage than men.

The liver metabolises (changes chemically) all but 10 per cent of the alcohol we drink. The first step is to change alcohol to acetaldehyde, a task done by liver enzymes. Then acetaldehyde is changed to acetic acid which leaves the liver, is dispersed through the body and broken down by other organs.

But when the liver has large amounts of alcohol to deal with it 'forgets' some of its other functions. Most of us who have had hangovers have experienced the unpleasant symptoms of nervousness, sweating, headache and trembling. This is because alcohol is not available to the body as sugar — despite the fact that it is made from sugar and high in calories — and furthermore, it interferes with the body's efforts to maintain a proper blood sugar level.

These hangover symptoms, together with hunger and weakness, are signs that the liver is failing to maintain normal blood sugar levels. Drinking on an empty stomach, or drinking so much with a meal that alcohol is still around after the food is digested, can bring on this state, known as hypoglycaemia. (It also partly accounts for the 'drinkers' munchies', that recurring desire for chips on the way home from the pub or chocolate biscuits the morning after.) Hypoglycaemia, if the body's sugar levels drop low enough, results in coma.

And the liver develops its own problems when repeatedly subjected to doses of alcohol. Normally, it 'burns' fat. But as soon as alcohol reaches the liver, it stops doing this and the fat content of the liver rises. The end result is a condition called 'fatty liver' which may cause other complications. Not just heavy drinkers, but moderate drinkers can develop fatty liver.

For as long as the liver is healthy it occupies a place just below the ribs in the upper right abdomen. If it becomes diseased, however, it can swell up and protrude from beneath the ribs.

For reasons connected with our immune system and metabolism, women are far more prone to liver disease — and in its severe and fatal forms — than men. Dr Roger Williams of Kings College Hospital has found that of his patients in the Liver Unit it is the women who suffer more often and have more severe liver damage from alcohol. He also finds that women are particularly likely to develop a form of inflammation of the liver known as alcoholic hepatitis.

The symptoms of this are fever, a high white blood-cell count, pain in the upper right abdomen and jaundice. It usually subsides when the patient stops drinking, but Dr Williams has found that in women, hepatitis is more likely to develop into cirrhosis and to end in early death. This is particularly true for women below forty-five years of age, or before the age of menopause. But if and how the menopause affects women's livers is not yet understood.

When liver damage becomes so severe that scarring occurs (and this can happen for reasons besides drinking such as infection), the liver ceases to function properly and cirrhosis develops. The liver fails in its task of removing impurities from the blood, the abdominal cavity may fill with fluid (dropsy) and the arms and legs become spindly. In men, the testes atrophy and breasts enlarge, while women stop menstruating and their breasts either enlarge or, more usually, shrink. If the disease is caught in time, these symptoms can be reversed, but if the drinker continues to take alcohol, cirrhosis can lead to death.

Cirrhosis was, until recently, generally considered to be a disease of elderly or middle-aged, heavily drinking men. But the numbers of women admitted to UK hospitals with the disease has increased about four-fold in the last decade and some 40 per cent of cirrhosis patients are now women.

Dr John Saunders, also of King's College Hospital Liver Unit, thinks women should be warned about the risks they take with alcohol at even low levels of drinking: 'Women may develop cirrhosis if their daily intake exceeds 40 grams of alcohol.' This is the equivalent of about two and a half pints of beer, four glasses of wine or two double measures of spirits — yet these are amounts that many women consider quite socially acceptable. (Men are not at risk until their daily intake exceeds 80 grams, according to Dr Saunders.)

Cirrhosis also develops more rapidly in women than in men: it takes on average thirteen years of excessive drinking for a woman to develop symptoms of cirrhosis, compared with twenty-two for a man.

Dr Sheila Sherlock of the Royal Free Hospital School of Medicine, puts the 'safe limit' for women even lower — at half the levels suggested by Dr Saunders. She estimates that 'as little as 20 grams of alcohol daily (about one and a half pints of beer, half a bottle of wine or two and a half measures of spirits) exposes the drinker to serious liver damage'. This, however, is her lowest 'safe' estimate and she sets a 'more realistic' average level of risk at 60 grams in women — as compared to about 80 for men.[4]

Fortunately, the liver does have an extraordinary capacity to function as required, even when up to two-thirds of its cells have been destroyed. It also has the power to replace its own damaged cells over a period of time. This is why 'binge' drinking seems to be less harmful to the liver than regular drinking, as the liver regenerates itself given a few 'days off'.

And not everyone who drinks excessively develops liver damage. The experts still don't know why but, according to Dr Sherlock, numerous 'chronic alcoholics [have] completely normal livers'.

YOUR HEART AND BLOOD STREAM

It is a popular — but false — notion that a good belt of alcohol will 'warm you up'. Pubs sell 'winter warmers' when the weather turns cold, and we are all familiar with the image of the friendly St Bernard dog, bringing sustenance in the form of brandy to freezing victims in the snow.

But although alcohol will make you *feel* warm temporarily by sending blood rushing to the skin capillaries, the end result is loss of body heat through the skin and so a lowering of temperature.

Alcohol increases blood flow to the brain, but in moderate amounts has only minor effects on heartbeat and blood pressure in most people. Angina sufferers do say, however, that a few drinks reduces the pain in their hearts, but this is probably the result of depression of the pain centres in the brain rather than of improved flow of blood to the heart.

In people suffering from ischaemic heart disease (lack of blood to the heart muscle) — which kills one-quarter of the UK population — moderate amounts of alcohol can produce arrhythmias, or lack of rhythm in the heart, which can lead to death.

Chronic drinking over many years will produce changes in the heart just as it does in the liver and nervous system. Because it is a poison, alcohol taken in large enough quantities kills the cells of the heart, causing a condition called cardiomyopathy. The heart dilates and grows massive in the attempt to replace the dead cells, but stops functioning efficiently. Heart failure and death can result.

On the positive side, there is some evidence that alcohol can prevent coronary disease, which is less common in the wine drinking countries than elsewhere.

As for the popular idea that a few drinks a day will help you relax and so keep heart trouble away, Dr Butler of the British Heart Foundation, says this is 'splitting hairs' ... 'There are so many factors involved in heart attacks that it is rubbish to say that a couple of gins a day are going to protect you.'

From another point of view, this could suggest that you might as well relax and enjoy a few drinks now and then ...

ALCOHOL AND OTHER DRUGS

Not only is women's drinking on the increase, but women's use of psychotropic drugs (drugs that affect the psyche, or conscious and unconscious mind — such as tranquillisers) has shot up in recent years. And because alcohol is a drug itself, its effects, when mixed with other drugs, can be particularly dangerous.

Estimates do vary, but women consume about twice as many psychotropic drugs as men. According to Dr Paul Williams of the Institute of Psychiatry, in the ten years after 1966, there was a 75 per cent overall increase in the numbers of prescriptions for anti-depressants and tranquillisers, and a 200 per cent increase in prescriptions for non-barbiturate hypnotics (sleeping pills).

Alcohol has a similar 'depressant' effect on your central nervous system to many other drugs, and so in combination the two can 'add' or 'multiply' each other's effects. It is worth asking your doctor and your chemist if you can safely drink while taking the drugs they dispense to you. (If you are appalled at the prospect of stopping drinking while a course of pills lasts, it is time for you to take a long hard look at your drinking habits: according to some definitions (see chapter 10) you have a 'problem'.)

Below are some of the more common drugs which, taken with alcohol, will 'add' to each other's depressant effects — with results varying from drowsiness, loss of coordination to coma and death:

Analgesics: these are painkillers like aspirin and paracetamol
Anti-histamines: these are drugs used against allergies, i.e. Phenergan, Piriton
Sedatives and tranquillisers: i.e. Valium, Librium and Largactil
Hypnotics: sleeping pills, such as Mogadon, and barbiturates
Anti-convulsants: these are prescribed to control fits, mainly epileptic, i.e. barbiturates, Phenytoin

When alcohol is mixed with barbiturates the effect can be especially dangerous and even lethal, as the two drugs multiply ('potentiate') each other's effect. The result of combining the two is therefore greater than the sum of the two doses.

When mixed with amphetamines, which are stimulants, alcohol can cause you to become excited or agitated and to behave in an unpredictable fashion.

If you take anti-depressants and drink, your coordination and concentration can suffer. And even a small amount of alcohol slows down the metabolism of other drugs so that they stay in your system longer.

Some drugs such as antibiotics (which stop the spread of infection, i.e. penicillin, tetracyclines) and anti-coagulants (these thin the blood and are used for heart trouble, i.e. warfarin, heparin), will be less effective in their therapeutic role if you drink while taking them.

Nor is it a good idea to mix drink with aspirin. Both of these drugs irritate the stomach lining and, if taken together, can cause bleeding in the stomach and difficulty in blood clotting. And don't take paracetamol with alcohol: you could seriously damage your liver.

ALCOHOL AND PREGNANCY

Drinking alcohol during pregnancy can damage the foetus and cause babies to be born with a broad range of mental and physical defects. The most severe combination of these is known as Foetal Alcohol Syndrome, or FAS, but just a couple of drinks a day can result in minor or undetected damage to the foetus so that babies may be born early, underweight or with some of the FAS symptoms.

WARNINGS FROM THE PAST

Taboos against drinking by would-be mothers and fathers date back to Old Testament times. 'You are barren and have no child, but you shall conceive and give birth to a son,' says the Angel of the Lord to a childless woman in the Book of Judges (13:7). 'Now you must do as I say: be careful to drink no wine or strong drink.'

In Carthage, bridal couples were banned from drinking on their wedding night in case they should conceive in a state of drunkenness and give birth to deformed children.[1]

And Aristotle, never renowned for his high opinion of women, wrote that 'foolish, drunken or hairbrain women for the most part bring forth children like unto themselves, morosos et languidos'.

In Britain, evidence of FAS was produced centuries ago: when James Sedgewick wrote *A New Treatise on Liquors* in 1725 he echoed Aristotle's tone in blaming women for the results of their drinking: 'Half of the train of chronical diseases with which we see children afflicted are only the secondary sighs and groanings, the evident marks and reproaches of parental ill-spent life... These consequences may, nay without doubt will be brought on infants, by the debauchery of the mother.' His conclusion was that women must be brought under control: 'The regulation of the mother during her pregnancy is an affair of the highest moment and consideration.'

The House of Commons heard evidence about alcohol's effects on the unborn as far back as 1834, when a select committee was told that babies of heavy drinking mothers tended to be born 'starved, shrivelled and imperfect in form'.[2]

Then in 1899, William Sullivan, a doctor to a Liverpool prison, reported the first case study of women who drank heavily in pregnancy. He found that the women 'drunkards' in the jail had an infant mortality and still-birth rate of 56 per cent — more than twice as high as that among their non-alcoholic female relatives.

He also found that some of the alcoholic women who had previously given birth to severely or even fatally damaged babies later gave birth to healthy children after being imprisoned — without drink — during pregnancy. Sullivan's conclusion was that 'maternal intoxication' was the chief source of damage to the foetus in these cases.[3]

THE PRESENT PICTURE

Only in the last decade has information been drawn together to pinpoint the syndrome which we now know as FAS. Most of the work has been done in America and Europe. But in the UK, despite pioneering work by individual researchers and doctors, government officials and the medical establishment have been extremely cautious to recognise the existence of FAS.

In consequence, many women in Britain don't know of the dangers of drinking during pregnancy. We all know about the hazards of smoking, and leaflets and posters have alerted women not to smoke when pregnant. But while the French and the Americans have launched major public health campaigns to warn pregnant women about drinking, British women are still more likely to have the attitude that 'a few drinks won't hurt'.

Early reports of the FAS phenomenon came from France in 1968 where researchers described 127 children of alcoholic women who had remarkably similar facial features and growth deficiencies.[4]

Five years later, *The Lancet* published a vital report of American research which showed that similar patterns of malformation in eight unrelated children born to alcoholic mothers had been found.[5] The children had similar facial features, growth deficiencies and mental retardation.

This report sparked off international interest, and in the following years, hundreds of case reports were published. Throughout the seventies more evidence emerged that alcohol could cause a broad spectrum of damage to the foetus. Dr Ann Streissguth, a leading researcher into FAS from the University of Washington, lists these as the chief risks to the foetus:[6]

— mental retardation
— retarded growth
— central nervous system abnormalities
— a variety of malformations
— death of the foetus within the uterus

IDENTIFYING FAS

Much of the controversy over FAS stems from the difficulties in recognising it. The features of the syndrome are *not* unique and can vary greatly in their severity. Malnutrition, smoking and other drugs may have similar effects to alcohol on the foetus. Because of this overlap, many doctors have thought that FAS symptoms were the result of Down's syndrome or some of the other disorders which share the FAS features.

But the accumulating evidence shows that when the full pattern of FAS is present, alcohol is always there in the mother's history. FAS has been recognised in babies *before* it was known that their mothers were alcoholic, whereas it has not been found in cultures where alcohol is not abused — even when the diet is very poor.[7]

And until we make a concerted effort to ensure that more women and doctors are aware of FAS, it will continue to go unrecognised — and unprevented.

Symptoms of FAS: FAS babies are typically underweight and small in body-length when born. They don't grow or develop well, and if seriously affected will not catch up mentally or physically with other babies. The mother — especially if she is drinking — may be blamed for the neglect of the child as it continues to look thin and ill. But even when hospitalised or taken into care the baby fares no better.[8]

Towards adolescence the child may put on more weight, but his or her IQ doesn't necessarily improve with age. FAS babies are generally mentally disabled with IQs ranging from 16 to 105, with a (mean) average of 65 (the national average is 100). As a baby he or she is often fractious, tremulous and has a feeble sucking response, and in childhood is likely to be hyperactive and a slow developer.

The 'cluster' of facial features which indicate FAS include a small head; shortened eyeslits; an underdeveloped upper lip; a short, snub nose; flattened profile and small chin. The eyelids may also be drooping and the eyes crossed.

Some of the vital organs can also be affected. Heart defects are common (about 30 per cent) in FAS babies, who may also have abnormal kidneys, slightly malformed genitals and abnormalities of the joints and palmar creases.[9]

It is important to stress that one by one these features may be hardly noticeable and may have nothing at all to do with FAS. Some of them occur for other reasons in babies of women who have never touched alcohol. But together these features form a characteristic 'constellation' which suggests FAS.

HOW ELSE DOES ALCOHOL AFFECT PREGNANCY AND CHILDBIRTH?

Even small amounts of alcohol can increase the risk of decreased birth weight, stillbirth and spontaneous abortion. Babies of 'social drinkers' can suffer from tremors and may not sleep well — even when they show no FAS symptoms.

Dr Streissguth has said that even an average of two drinks a day during pregnancy could nearly double the chances that a baby will be stillborn, be smaller than normal, or will suffer from some other congenital defect.[10]

And babies who are born with a low birth weight are prone to early health problems and vulnerable to infections. Babies born with FAS symptoms may have the same problems of withdrawal from alcohol as adults, experiencing tremors, irritability, spontaneous seizures and increased respiration rate.

Drinking alcohol at the time of childbirth and during breastfeeding can also be harmful to the child. Women sometimes take alcohol to relieve the pain of labour or to hold back premature labour. But the alcohol will pass into the baby's blood, adversely affecting its breathing, central nervous system and bone cells.

Many nursing mothers are also advised by doctors that having a drink will help them to relax. Yet not only does alcohol appear in the breast milk, but the process of ejecting it from the breast can be slowed down by alcohol.[11]

American researchers have also found a relationship between alcoholism and a high incidence of gynaecological and obstetric problems such as infertility, miscarriages and hysterectomy.[12] But which of these problems comes first, or causes the other, is not yet understood.

Very little research has been done into the effects of alcohol on male sperm and its possible consequent affect on the foetus. But it is known that drink is a testicular toxin and heavy drinking in men (five or more drinks a day) can result in reduced production of sperm and production of abnormal sperm.

HOW DOES ALCOHOL DAMAGE THE FOETUS?

Until about the 1940s, scientists thought that the uterus was virtually unaffected by harmful substances in the mother's body — but in the early sixties the thalidomide tragedy changed those ideas once and for all. And now alcohol has joined the long list of 'environmental' agents with the potential to damage the foetus.

No one yet knows exactly how FAS, or other alcohol-related birth defects, are caused. It is not known *when* or in what *quantity* drink will affect the foetus. Researchers are still trying to discover why some babies and not others are affected: twins have been born, one with and one without FAS symptoms.

Nor do we know whether the mechanisms of FAS work exclusively through the mother, or whether the father's drinking can result in a malformed foetus if the father's sperm is affected by alcohol at the time of conception.

SAFE LIMITS: IS IT TRUE THAT 'A FEW DRINKS WON'T HURT'?

There is no agreement about the safe limits of drinking during pregnancy — and this is the hottest area of the dispute about FAS. But more and more medical experts are coming to the conclusion that pregnant women and women likely to conceive *should not drink at all.*

In Britain, the Royal College of Psychiatrists has said that 'even very moderate social drinking may be associated with decreased birth weight and increased risk of spontaneous abortion'.[13]

Although it is difficult to put a figure on exactly how many drinks may be dangerous, say the College, 'the woman who is drinking "alcoholically" is certainly putting her baby at risk, but it is possible that lesser degrees of deformity may occur even with more moderate drinking'.

Their conclusion is clear: 'Pregnant women would be well advised not to drink alcohol during pregnancy.'

American health officials have been saying so — and much more emphatically — for years. 'For baby's sake and yours, don't drink during pregnancy' is the message of a massive publicity campaign launched by the American National Institute on Alcohol Abuse and Alcoholism (NIAAA).

This followed the first official government warning that alcohol could damage the foetus. The US Surgeon General issued a statement in July 1981 advising women who are pregnant or considering pregnancy not only to abstain from alcohol, but to 'be aware of the alcoholic content of food and drugs'.

Rather than trying to draw the line at a certain level of drinking, some medical experts say we should regard alcohol as potentially damaging in any case and this damage as increasing by degree.

There is no 'threshold effect' of safety for any teratogen (any substance which can damage the foetus) yet studied in humans, according to Dr David Smith.[14] None of these substances are safe to a particular level and dangerous only beyond that.

The unequivocal stand taken by the Americans is based on years of research. One Boston Medical School study, reported by the National Council of Women, compared the health of babies born to heavy, moderate and occasional drinkers (heavy drinking was defined as more than three spirit measures, three glasses of wine or a pint and half of beer).[15]

Babies of the 'heavy drinkers' were found to be 'worse off ... by almost every criterion': many of them suffered from jittery nerves, poor muscle tone, had low birth weights, small heads, were premature and showed more 'major, minor and multiple congenital anomalies'. Many of them had difficulty in sucking.

The Boston researchers concluded that the only way to stop alcohol-related birth defects appearing in babies (apart from abortion) is to cut down on drink. Two-thirds of the women in the Boston study who did so had normal babies. But all of the babies — except two — born to the heavy drinkers who did not cut down were 'abnormal'.

Other eminent American researchers have been saying for years that pregnant women, to be safe, should *not drink at all.*

Dr Ruth Little, Director of the Alcoholism and Drug Abuse Institute at the University of Washington, says that regular social drinking (two or more drinks daily) is linked with retarded growth of the foetus and behavioural problems in the baby — as well as low birth weight and still-birth.[16]

British doctors have confirmed these views. Three measures of spirits or a pint and a half of beer may seriously impair the growth of the foetus, according to Dr Balfour Sclare of Duke Street Hospital in Glasgow.[17] And Dr David Woollam of Cambridge University, consultant to the World Health Organization since the thalidomide disaster, has said that pregnant women should avoid alcohol completely.[18]

AVERSIONS

For some women 'safe limits' is never an issue: they simply cannot face alcohol when pregnant. Many women suffer from morning sickness (usually connected to a healthy pregnancy) and feel too sick to drink. At the same time, some women lose all desire for cigarettes and coffee, substances which can also be bad for the foetus.

The biological reason for these aversions is not fully understood, but 'pregnancy is the only life event' writes Dr Ruth Little, '(for either males or females) associated with a spontaneous, predictable and substantial decrease in alcohol use'. Even heavy drinkers tend to drink less when they get pregnant — and, again according to Dr Little, they tend to cut down even before they realise they are pregnant.[19]

But cutting down on drinking is very difficult for women who are dependent on alcohol, whether they are pregnant or not. All the more reason for education about the risks of drinking, long before women even think of having a baby.

WHEN ARE YOU AT RISK?

It could be that *when* you drink has an important effect on pregnancy. One theory is that the first three months are a critical time when alcohol can be particularly harmful.

Before most women even realise they are pregnant in their fourth week, some vital developments have taken place in the foetus. By eight weeks most of the major organs have begun to develop.

Between the third and the fifth months the brain develops very fast, and this is another period when the foetus could be prone to damage.

Another theory is that there could be a particular critical period during pregnancy when the foetus is especially vulnerable to damage from alcohol. This might explain why babies with FAS features have been born to mothers who had just a few drinks now and then, as well as to women who drank rarely but heavily.

It could also be that hereditary factors determine whether, and when, a foetus is vulnerable.

THE SIZE OF THE PROBLEM: HOW MANY PREGNANCIES ARE AT RISK?

FAS is thought by some to occur at least once in every 1,000 births, but 'partial manifestations of the syndrome are much more common and occur possibly once in every 300 births' — which is why 'it is considered the major preventable birth defect'.[20]

This represents a huge toll of suffering — especially in the light of the American NIAAA statement that FAS is the third leading cause of mental retardation, and neurological problems in babies (only Down's syndrome and Spina Bifida are more prevalent). The NIAAA estimate that one in every 2,000 babies born in the USA each year displays all the FAS characteristics.

Dr David Smith has said that alcohol is the 'most frequent known teratogenic cause of mental deficiency in the western world'.[21] And Dr Little believes that one in ten pregnancies may be at some risk from alcohol although not all children at risk will show any effects.

The estimates of how many babies are at risk vary between different countries and different studies. In the UK, Dr David Woollam, Director of Studies in Medicine at Emmanuel College and Peterhouse, Cambridge, and an authority on mammalian teratology, has estimated that 1,000 babies a year are born with FAS and that about 10 per cent of all malformations (in the US and the UK) are due to 'maternal alcoholism'.[22] His estimate puts the risk from alcoholism to the foetus *higher* than the risk of Down's syndrome.

These figures, however, remain estimates until such time as our government and medical establishment put more resources into research and education on FAS. In the meantime, we don't know which groups of women are most at risk during pregnancy in the UK, although it is well established that poverty and low social class increase a baby's chance of being born small and of dying in the perinatal period (from the seventh month of pregnancy to the first week of life). Working-class women have a higher chance of having smaller babies and babies who will die from malformations than middle-class women.[23]

The risks to the foetus from alcohol have to be seen in the context of this much greater overall problem of poverty (which our government chooses to ignore, giving priority to spending on weapons). Foresight, the association for the promotion of pre-conceptual care, estimate that between 6 and 10 per cent of all children have some disability at the age of five years. They claim that up to half of these arise in the perinatal period and could have been prevented.[24]

Alcohol is just one of the 'social poisons' responsible for this tragic toll, which could have been reduced through education, good nutrition and protection from pollutants — as well as through avoiding cigarettes and alcohol. Many factors in western life combine to deplete our bodies of essential vitamins and trace minerals. This 'hidden malnutrition' — not always evident in the parents — places the foetus at risk, say Foresight. Zinc for example, is important to a foetus's healthy development, but alcohol consumption (as well as the contraceptive pill, copper piping in soft water areas, the refining and processing of foods and the use of chemical fertilisers) cheats our bodies of it.[25]

Foresight has also been one of the few groups to say that the father's health in the conception of a healthy foetus has been too long overlooked, although it is a principal well established in farming and animal breeding. So far the emphasis has been on a mother's responsibility for a healthy pregnancy and she is made to carry the burden of guilt for any failures. But Foresight say *both* parents should ideally be well nourished and free from toxic substances, such as alcohol, before they try to conceive.

The personal, social and economic costs of disability are high, but the suffering of mother and child, and the tragedy of lost potential for FAS children can never be calculated. Until the government decides to make education and prevention a priority, it is a tragedy which will continue.

9

HANGOVERS: 'THE WRATH OF GRAPES'

The hangover is not simply a physical state which follows over-indulgence in alcohol. For some drinkers it has a semi-mystical significance — it is their badge of boozing courage, and is almost as important as getting drunk. But for others it is an occasion for excruciating guilt, remorse and sickness, the stigma of shameful behaviour.

Women (see chapters 1 and 2) are particularly prone to regrets about loss of control and waste of time.

Men, far more than women, are likely to get a kick out of their hangovers, just as they are usually more proud of their drinking exploits. The hangover, especially amongst a group of men who have been drinking together, brings with it a kind of macho, locker-room spirit, the cameraderie of battle survivors. Men who have gone 'over the top' together are inclined to relish their shared symptoms the next morning, comparing the state of their heads, stomachs and bowels.

David Outerbridge has written *The Hangover Handbook* in this vein, and it is full of jokey anecdotes, caricatures of men with big noses and squiffy eyes, and 'cures' — such as this one from Kingsley Amis:[1] 'Upon awakening: If your wife or other partner is beside you, and (of course) is willing, perform the sexual act as vigorously as you can. The exercise will do you good, and — on the assumption that you enjoy sex — you will feel toned up emotionally.'

In the same spirit is a quote from the notorious drinking 'hero' W.C. Fields as he refuses a chaser of water: 'Watah — fish fuck in water.' Fields' hangover cure is more booze — a martini of one part vermouth and four parts of gin, 'to be taken around the clock'.

And it is not only our culture that finds the hangover funny. David Outerbridge translates the phrases used in other countries to show how evocative the expressions can be:

French: *gueule de bois*, snout of wood
German: *Katzenjammer*, a wailing of cats
Norwegian: *jeg har tommermenn*, I have carpenters in my head
Italian: *stonato*, out of tune

Portugese: *ressaca,* literally undertow, or line of surf, or 'the tide has gone out'.[2]

His own description has all the masochistic gusto of the true hangover connoisseur:

The head is an urn of complaints. Most immediate is a hammering headache that is both dull and intense simultaneously. To move the head causes new pains at the back of the skull, and to open the eyes sends shafts of painful light in the front. The ears ring and outside noises are unusually abrasive. The mouth is dry and feels caked. The taste is terrible and breath feels foul (and is). The tongue and throat are parched, the chest is taut with heartburn, and any attempt to move causes severe dizziness. This sensation of queasiness immediately telegraphs itself to the stomach which is entertaining its own disorders. The dizziness compounds a feeling of general nausea; sometimes this will surge into a fit of vomiting, but more often will continue to hold the victim in a limbo of wooziness and diarrhoea, and a desire for a cathartic heave. In addition, the stomach walls have been scoured by the alcohol, producing true indigestion. The nervous system is still drugged, causing the body to experience uncontrolled shakes: this is most noticeable in the hands, but the flushes of the face and the chills of the torso are allied manifestations.

The author is showing off, but habitual drinkers will recognise some of these disorders.

In more prosaic terms the symptoms of a hangover can include digestive upsets (vomiting, loss of appetite, heartburn), emotional upsets (anxiety, depression), thirst, weakness, headache, sweating, giddiness, general shakiness and tremor of the eyeballs, palpitations, and fatigue.

This is how your body makes its protest when you have inflicted too much drink upon it. Alcohol is directly poisonous to the tissues and your body can only eliminate it at a constant rate. If you drink too much and/or too fast you will 'overload' it and the ill effects of alcohol will accumulate.

And in addition to the toxic effects of alcohol, the body has to cope with other impurities in alcoholic drinks called congeners. These are substances which may derive from yeasts, sugars, flavourings and colourings in alcoholic beverages. The closer your type of drink is to pure alcohol, the less congeners it should contain. Vodka for instance is purer than bourbon whisky, and white wine has less congeners than red wine.

It is thought that a number of hangover symptoms are the result of allergic reactions to congeners[3] and it is worth bearing this in mind if you are counting your drinks in terms of units. The alcohol content of six units of beer (three pints) will be the same as the alcohol content of six units of red wine (six glasses). The damage done by the alcohol will be the same for both drinks, but you may feel worse if you drink the wine, as a result of the different congeners.

SYMPTOMS

Hangover symptoms vary considerably according to the individual, the kind of drink taken, how much of it you consume and how accustomed you are to drinking. But the lowest common denominator of the hangover is probably tiredness.

Tiredness: You could be tired simply because you were drinking until the small hours and got up early, and so haven't had enought time asleep.

But if you go to bed drunk, the quality of your sleep is poor anyway and you are likely to wake up unrefreshed. This is because you have missed vital Rapid Eye Movement (REM) sleep, so called because the eyes move rapidly under the lids, 'watching' the events of your dream.

Studies have shown that for our physical and mental health we all need to experience this form of 'dreaming' sleep. Without it, people can become extremely irritable and anxious.

REM sleep normally occurs four or five times a night for periods of half an hour. But for this to happen the higher brain needs to be very active and if it has been 'numbed' by alcohol (or sleeping pills) you cannot have REM sleep until the anaesthetic effect has worn off. This can take several hours — depending on how much you have consumed, and so the value of your sleep is less than you might normally expect.

Some drinkers try to sleep long into the morning to make up for their lost dreaming time, but it is a common complaint of hangover victims that they wake up feeling anxious and guilty at the crack of dawn and can't get back to sleep.

Your fatigue from a poor sleep is likely to be further aggravated by sheer bodily tiredness, the results of overdoing it while drunk the night before. It is a common pattern to feel tired in the evening after a busy day, and to have a few drinks to perk you up. With this new-found but artificial energy (the drink has numbed the parts of the brain which register physical discomfort and weariness), you continue to go on drinking. If you feel sufficiently revived you might go on to a party — drinking, talking, dancing and generally over-exerting yourself. You feel the effects of this the next day as the alcoholic anaesthesia wears off, the pain centres of the brain wake up and your body feels as if you had put it through a wringer.

Headache: You are also likely to have a headache. This could be a consequence of tiredness, of dehydration or of falling asleep in an awkward position. It could also be an allergic reaction to the congeners found in drinks like port, sherry or red wine.

According to David Outerbridge, the brain cell walls have adapted to alcohol by becoming more sensitive — hence the hyper-sensitivity of your head on the morning after. He says the solution is to allow the brain cells to return to normal, by taking a small quantity of alcohol or 'the hair of the dog'. This avoids the 'abrupt, disquieting shock' of the return to normal and the consequent headache.[4] This is a popular theory in the macho tradition, but one which conflicts with the arguments of the medical specialists, who say that most of all your body now needs a complete rest from alcohol. Fighting booze with booze is a dangerous practice, and if you reach the stage where only drink can alleviate your hangover symptoms you are entering the vicious circle of alcohol dependence.

Thirst: Habitual drinkers will be familiar with another sure sign of having overdone it — waking up in the night or morning with a raging thirst.

This happens partly because alcohol, by acting on the hormones which control production of urine, makes you urinate more than usual. But alcohol also alters the distribution of water in your body, pulling liquid out of the cells and increasing the amount of extra-cellular fluid. The thirst you feel is in response to the need to replenish your body cells.

You can stave off some of the ill effects of dehydration by drinking plenty of water before you go to sleep.

Digestive upsets: Swallow too much of anything and your stomach will rebel; alcohol is no exception. *How much* is too much, your insides are likely to signal to you at the time — which is why vomiting plays a large part in drinking stories, especially for beginner drinkers.

If you are a regular drinker the ill effects are less likely to make themselves felt until the following morning. Queasiness is consequently a common hangover symptom. The prospect of putting food into your ravaged stomach is repulsive, and if your hangover is severe you may vomit when you get moving in the morning.

Even after vomiting you may still feel nauseous and bilious, or suffer an attack of the dreaded 'dry heaves', in which you go through the motions of vomiting but nothing happens because your stomach is empty. You may not be able to face food for some time.

If you resort to drink as a 'cure', or start drinking again before replenishing your body with food and allowing your digestive tract to recover, you are likely to upset the mechanisms of appetite and nutrition and suffer from vitamin deficiency. Chronic drinking eventually interferes with the process of digesting and absorbing food and chronic gastritis can be the result. Continuous stomach upsets are one of the warning signs of problem drinking.

Emotional upsets: As unpleasant as the physical symptoms of a hangover can be, they are bearable, to some extent treatable — and you know that in time they will pass. But the mental and emotional suffering that can accompany a hangover is a far more distressing experience.

Guilt, depression, remorse, shame and self-accusation often comprise the legacy of a drinking bout. When this happens the hangover sufferer wakes up in the morning (probably at dawn and wracked with anxiety), recalls what happened the night before and swears never to touch another drop. For reasons already described, this is more likely to happen to women than to men.

For men, the hangover can be simply the consequence of sociable masculine behaviour, the mark of being 'one of the lads', and nothing to be ashamed of. But for women, getting drunk is not generally socially acceptable. Drunken behaviour in women is frowned upon, associated with 'promiscuity' and 'unfeminine' comportment. The drunk woman may have escaped these strictures for as long as she is drinking, but when she is sober again — and physically unwell from the hangover — all the weight of social and internalised condemnation descends on her head.

It is also generally true that women have more to *do* than men. The division between work and leisure time doesn't exist in many women's lives — either because their work *is* in the home, or because their work continues in the home when they return from their paid jobs. For women then, 'wasting time' with a hangover is a more serious and guilt-ridden business than it is for most men.

You may also have said or done things when drunk which you later regret and so feel guilty or ashamed. If you are one of those people who swear to go on the wagon after every binge, you will be further depressed by the 'failure' to keep your resolutions — especially if your drinking upsets other people who are close to you.

But if you do feel depressed and upset after a drinking bout, try to remember that your physiological state is also magnifying your emotional pain. Anxiety and depression are well-recognised symptoms of heavy drinking, and the way you feel about yourself could be as much a consequence of chemical changes in your body, as of what you have done or said.

Take some rest and concentrate on getting your body back into shape before examining your conscience too rigorously. And try to put your social embarrassment into the context of the double standard for men and women drinkers.

PREVENTION AND CURE

The only sure way to prevent a hangover is — don't drink. But if you want to drink, or think you might be put in a social situation where it is difficult to refuse, there are several things you can do to make the following day easier for yourself:

— Try to drink slowly, sipping instead of gulping drinks. If you arrive at the pub or party feeling very parched, quench your thirst first with a few soft drinks before starting on alcohol.

Try to keep your consumption down to one unit of alcohol (i.e. one glass of wine or half a pint of beer) per hour. By drinking more or faster than this you are likely to become increasingly intoxicated until you abandon all the good resolutions of your sober self — and feel the consequences in the morning.

— Eat something, preferably fatty or oily food or drink milk, before you start drinking alcohol. The food will line the walls of your stomach and intestine, slowing the rate of absorption of alcohol.

— Stop drinking alcohol several hours before you are expecting to go to sleep and have another snack of food and drink some water, fruit juice or other soft drinks. If you are feeling queasy, take some liver salts before going to bed.

— There are many old adages about the dangers of drinking different types of alcohol in one sitting ('Don't mix the grape and the grain'), and some of the worst hangovers strike after all the beer or wine has run out and people start drinking whatever else they can lay their hands on, usually spirits.

On these occasions it is probably the sheer quantity of alcohol consumed that does most of the damage, but most drinkers agree that it is safer to stick to one kind of drink.

It is a well-established custom, however, to mix drinks, starting with an aperitif, then wine, etc. on stylish occasions structured around a meal. In this case the small dose of each drink, the length of time taken over the meal and the food itself, help blot up the ill-effects.

— Sleep for as long as you can to make up for those lost hours of refreshing REM sleep. If you do wake up early feeling anxious, try to go back to sleep if you can. It sometimes helps to get up for a while and have a hot drink and a bath. Or do something 'virtuous' like tidying up — and then go back to bed. If you can't sleep during the morning, make sure your next night is an early one.

CURES

The search for the hangover miracle cure has yielded countless remedies, recipes and potions. Some of these are common sense; others are plain harmful.

The only sure remedy is to stop drinking alcohol, drink plenty of fluids, get some rest and *wait*. You have put poisons into your body and you must give it time to recover. But in the meantime there are things you can do to make yourself feel better.

— Painkillers, like aspirin, will help your headache or other aches, but might also further irritate your stomach. You can avoid this by sticking to the soluble brands.

— Replenish your body with vitamins and minerals. Alcohol can eventually deplete the body's store of minerals such as magnesium, calcium and potassium. Lack of magnesium can cause cramps and spasms and irritability of the nerves and muscles. A dose of liver salts or magnesium sulphate will help remedy this deficiency.

Lack of potassium can cause tremors. Eat oranges and tomatoes to make up for this. For calcium, drink milk and eat cheese, sardines, herrings, flour and watercress.

Alcohol also runs down your supply of vitamins B_1, B_6 and C. Foods rich in the B vitamins are wholemeal bread, yeast, dairy products and meats like liver and bacon. Vitamin C is best taken in the form of citrus fruits or their juices, green vegetables, blackcurrants and new potatoes. B and C vitamins can usually be bought in tablet form, and it is quite a good idea for regular drinkers to take these as a matter of course.

— Fresh air and exercise can help you to feel better generally by getting your blood circulation moving so that reviving oxygen is carried around the body. (A whiff of pure oxygen is also said to work wonders, but is not available to most of us.)

Psychologically, exercise can be especially helpful. You will feel you are doing something healthy to make up for the damage inflicted on your body — and the activity helps to relieve stress and calm the nerves if you are suffering from hangover guilt.

But don't overdo it; you are likely to be tired and your body might get more benefit from rest. The type of exercise which gets the circulation going and relaxes without exhausting you, like yoga or some gentle swimming, is ideal.

— There are some so-called cures which might give you an instant lift, but which won't do you any good in the long run. Coffee, for instance, will help wake you up and slake your thirst, and it is soothing as a hot drink. But it is no more a miraculous remedy for a hangover than it is a good way to sober up. Strong coffee especially can make you even more anxious and jittery when your nerves are bad, and it can make stomach acidity worse.

Again, many hardened drinkers swear by the 'hair of the dog' — another dose of alcohol. But this habit has probably helped them to become hardened drinkers in the first place. A couple of drinks on the morning after — if you can face them — might well make you feel better *temporarily*. The alcohol will anaesthetise some of your painful symptoms, and in topping up your blood alcohol level again, you are averting the unpleasantness of withdrawal from the drug.

But this is *not* an advisable practice. Your liver and other organs need time to recover before they face another onslaught of alcohol. And the more you drink the more your level of tolerance is likely to rise, and the higher your chances of becoming a dangerously dependent drinker. In the long run it will be much better for you to ride out the withdrawal symptoms or alleviate them with some of the above methods.

Some doctors say you should abstain altogether for several days — and others say weeks — before taking any more drink on board.

DO YOU HAVE A DRINKING PROBLEM?

We have a whole range of words to describe the use and abuse of alcohol such as 'heavy' drinking, 'moderate' and 'social' drinking, 'problem' drinking and 'alcoholism'. They are morally weighted and ill-defined words: a judgement is implicit in each of them, and my idea of a heavy drinker might be your idea of an alcoholic, or vice versa.

Yet the imprecise nature of these terms reflects the variable and shifting nature of drinking patterns and problems. To be a drinker is to stand somewhere on a continuum: at one extreme is problem-free abstinence, at the other is the complex of drinking problems usually called 'alcoholism.'

WHAT DOES 'ALCOHOLISM' MEAN? — THE LONG-STANDING DEBATE

The argument about the meaning of alcoholism has been a long and heated one. Politicians, brewers, social workers, doctors, drinkers, all have some kind of interest in the 'correct' definition — and so the debate goes on. Different theories have held sway at different times, and have had a crucial effect on the treatment of people with alcohol problems.

In recent decades in this country, the concept of alcoholism as a *disease* prevailed, and alcoholics were the domain of the medical profession. It was generally believed that the reasons a person got into trouble with alcohol were due to that individual's biochemistry or personality. Alcoholics were thought to have some abnormality which made them unable to control their drinking, so that abstinence was the only 'cure'. (Alcoholics Anonymous (AA), has remained faithful to this idea, their members attempting to 'get sober' permanently, yet continuing to call themselves alcoholics — people who are 'allergic' to alcohol.)

The disease concept helped to lighten the burden of moral judgement against alcoholics who had in previous times been condemned for weakness and sinfulness, and justified their treatment as people who needed support and rehabilitation rather than punishment. But this theory was limited: it implied that there could be one explanation for *all* alcoholism. However, years of research has come up with no evidence of any single personality or biochemical factor that alone could cause alcoholism.

In recent years, increasing recognition has been given to the relationship between alcohol problems and the *per capita* consumption of alcohol in any population. It was found that those societies which drank the most also had the most alcoholics and the most deaths from cirrhosis. Drink problems were attributed to the *amount* consumed in any society. But this theory again left out certain important questions. Why, for instance, did some people and not others in the same society come to grief through alcohol?

Opinion in the alcohol field is still divided. Broadly speaking, there are two main camps. One takes the medical model, talks about alcoholism as a disease, and recommends abstinence as a 'cure'. The other stresses the social context of drinking and believes that 'problem drinkers' (rather than 'alcoholics'), can learn to control their drinking without necessarily abstaining.

But the years of dispute have led to a concensus that alcoholism is a highly complex phenomenon with no single cause or 'cure'. The evidence of recent years is that there are many different factors — social, economic, psychological and physiological — involved in problem drinking. This wide range of factors affects why, what and when we drink, and also how much harm will result.

Authorities like the World Health Organization now tend to avoid the term 'alcoholism' and use 'dependence on alcohol' or 'alcohol-dependence syndrome'. The term alcoholism is widely felt to be unsatisfactory as it implies *one* disease instead of the many types of alcohol abuse which exist, and the range of problems which lie behind them.

Where the term is still used, it is used for convenience and is broadly defined: 'Repeated consumption of alcohol leading to dependence, physical disease or other harm' is a typical definition.[1] Alcoholism is seen as a condition not only related to the *amounts* of drink consumed; also important is the drinker's social background, health, diet, work and pattern of drinking.

Workers in the alcohol field now seem less concerned with precise definitions than with the practical implications of the terminology. For instance, some say they find 'alcoholism' useful in describing extreme drinking problems; others avoid it because of the stigma attached. For women in particular the label 'alcoholic' can be damaging, further lowering a woman's self-esteem and discouraging her from coming forward for treatment. ACCEPT argue that calling a person 'alcoholic' confirms her in a 'loser's role' which she may have subconsciously chosen, and so perpetuates her drinking problems.

And unless 'alcoholism' is understood in its full complexity, its causes cannot effectively be tackled. 'A treatment approach which is narrowly conceived in terms of such simple propositions as, for example, alcoholism is *always* rooted in personality disorder, *always* due to lack of social skills, or *always* the result of loneliness, is likely to be inadequate and misconceived.'[2]

THE PREVAILING THEORY

In recent years, opinion in the alcohol field has moved towards a multidimensional approach. Factors of class, sex and race greatly affect our drinking patterns. Current understanding of alcohol problems follows broadly along these lines: Initially, the pattern of our drinking is affected by cultural attitudes. In some cultures drinking is seen as 'manly' behaviour, whereas in others it is forbidden. In our society, drinking is accepted by the majority as a sociable form of behaviour for adults, but drunkenness is less acceptable, especially in women.

We learn to drink within this framework of 'informal social controls',[3] and under varying degrees of social pressure we develop our drinking 'habit'. There are certain high-risk occupations (such as bar work and journalism), and groupings (young males), in which the pressure to drink is especially strong.

Having a parent with drink problems also significantly increases our chances of developing problems. Both the environmental effect of 'learned behaviour' from parents who we see using booze to 'cope' with their difficulties, and hereditary factors, contribute to this. As yet there is no definite evidence that a physical predisposition to alcohol dependence can be inherited. It does seem likely, however, that a genetic susceptibility which makes individuals more vulnerable to the effects of alcohol could be one of the many factors involved in drinking problems.[4]

Depression can also lead to the drinker developing problems (although not much is known about this). Women, for instance, are more likely than men to turn to professional counsellors, therapists, and antidepressant drugs when they feel distressed. Men are more likely to resort to alcohol than to seek professional help. And the more education you have, the more likely you are to seek professional help rather than the short-term benefits of alcohol.[5]

Below a certain level of drinking, no physical dependency should develop, but psychological dependency can develop after a period (several years or even months) of having a regular drink. We feel we 'need' a drink when it comes to our usual time for having one. If we don't have one we feel as uncomfortable as a smoker who is trying to give up cigarettes. But at this stage there would be no physical withdrawal symptoms if we did give up. This psychological dependence reinforces our learned habit, and the more we drink, the stronger these factors become.

The extent of drinking at this level is also affected by the price and availability of drink. If you have enough spare cash, if you work in a traditionally boozy job, if the price of drink is low and the pub opening hours long, you are likely to drink more than you would under different circumstances.

Eventually alcohol's properties as a drug which induces physical dependence begin to take effect, and your body's response to alcohol becomes different from what it was initially. It is now thought that *anybody*, under certain circumstances, could become physically dependent on alcohol, but the major factors are how much a person drinks and for how long.

Although the critical amount varies from one individual to another, physical dependence (and chronic physical damage) can develop in a woman when she is consuming forty grams of alcohol or more each day, according to Dr John Saunders of Kings College Hospital Liver Unit. (Forty grams is the equivalent of more than two pints of beer, two double whiskies, or four glasses of wine.) Physical dependence is however 'unusual' below sixty grams but women can become physically damaged without developing dependence.

Once the drinker has become dependent it takes more and more alcohol to achieve the same level of intoxication, and without continuous doses of drink she or he will suffer withdrawal symptoms such as shakiness, sweating and anxiety. Below is a list of the symptoms of alcohol dependence in the order in which they most commonly occur:[6]

Completely unable to keep to a drink limit
Need more drink than companions (i.e. going for drink between rounds)
Difficulty preventing getting drunk
Spending more time drinking
Missing meals drinking
'Blackouts', memory loss
Giving up interests because drinking interferes

Restless without a drink
Changes to drinking same on working days as on days off
Organising day to ensure supply
Change to drinking same amounts whatever mood
Passing out from drink in public
Trembling after drinking the day before
Times when can't think of anything except getting a drink
Morning retching or vomiting
Sweating excessively at night
Withdrawal fit
Morning drinking
Decreased tolerance
Waking up panicking or frightened
Hallucinations

Unfortunately, it is a well-known characteristic of developing alcohol dependence that the drinker tends to deny that any problem exists. The drinking continues and increases as long as health and circumstances permit.

Anger, threats, pleas and accusations can often have no effect other than reinforcing the drinker's sense of isolation and guilt, and adding to the 'reasons' for drinking. All too often it takes a major disaster — a partner leaving, getting the sack, or health collapsing — before she or he seeks treatment.

TACKLING THE PROBLEM

Most professional treatment agencies are geared to dealing with the results only of extreme drinking problems. Alcoholics Anonymous, too, is generally a last resort for alcoholics. Very few organisations offer help *before* major damage is done (with exceptions like Drinkwatchers, see below).

This is partly because denial is a common factor in drinking problems, and partly because the 'responsible' bodies in this country (some of which have vested interests in *not* reducing alcohol consumption, see chapter 6) put so few resources into prevention and education.

For these reasons, women who fear they are developing, or could develop, alcohol problems will have difficulty in finding an established agency geared to their needs. If this is your situation, you may decide that self-help is your best option.

SELF HELP

As the all-women groups run by professional workers have shown, we can gain enormously from joint discussion and mutual support. Our sense of guilt over drinking can be alleviated in a group where other women feel they have been drinking too much, or admit that they too have taken to drinking secretly or hiding bottles around the house.

And as there is no way of understanding the reasons why we drink without becoming aware of our situation as women in society, self-help groups can help us to identify common areas of discontent and frustration as a first step towards dealing with them — without depending on drink.

You may want to organise your group amongst friends, or through a local women's centre. Alternatively, try putting an advertisement in the free listings of a magazine, *Spare Rib* for instance.

I would suggest four main areas of discussion for a drinkers' self-help group: why do you drink, how much do you drink, what kind of a drinker are you, and strategies for cutting down.

Why do you drink?: The group could talk about reasons for drink in general terms. Do you abuse alcohol when you are feeling shy or angry, frustrated or lonely, or when under stress? If so, what are the circumstances and situations which make you feel this way? Try to work out new ways of coping with stress (such as exercise or yoga), or techniques of avoiding it (perhaps assertiveness training).

How much do you drink?: Work out how much you are in the habit of drinking. Add up the number of drinks you have had every day for a typical week, using the basic unit of one for a glass of wine or sherry, a pub tot of spirits or half pint of beer or lager. (Cans of special strength lager count as three units each.)

This unit system is a convenient way of working out the alcohol content of whatever you are drinking, and the damage done by the alcohol in four units of whisky and four units of beer will be the same. Bear in mind, however, that some drinks have additional dangers. If you drink spirits, especially at home, you are likely to pour larger measures than you would get in a pub, and do yourself more harm. And you can drink whisky much faster than beer and so get more drunk, more quickly. Beer however, is unit-for-unit more fattening than spirits, which can make for further health and emotional problems. And some drinks, such as red wine, have more congeners and may give you worse hangovers.

Don't be discouraged if your total of units seems alarmingly high at first, or higher than anyone else's. Cutting down can be a slow process, so give yourself credit for every bit of progress.

Your eventual target should be about twenty units a week, or three units a day, or even less. Allow yourself a bit more leeway if you don't drink everyday; 'days off' in between drinking give your body time to recover and replenish itself.

What kind of drinker are you?: The following questions (based on a London Council on Alcoholism questionnaire), are designed to help you assess your drinking pattern in terms of dependency and vulnerability to problems. Put a tick against the statements which are true, or closest to the truth for you. Tick one for each category, and then add up your score as shown below:

1. If I was advised to give up drinking for the sake of my health —
a. I could do so easily
b. I could do so but I'd miss it
c. I could do so but with difficulty
d. I could only do so if I had help
e. I don't think I could do it

2. This time last year my favourite drink was —
a. stronger than what I drink now
b. weaker than what I drink now
c. the same as what I drink now

3. When I am drinking with my friends I notice that —
a. they seem to drink about the same speed that I do
b. they drink faster than I do
c. some of them drink slower than I do
d. most of them drink slower than I do

If you answered yes to a or b, also answer the following:
e. I have changed my friends
f. I have kept my old friends

If you answered yes to e, then also answer the following:
   My new friends —
g. drink faster than my old friends
h. drink slower than my old friends

4. Where I buy my drink —
a. I have a credit account
b. I do not have a credit account

If you answered yes to a, then also answer the following:
   The amount that I owe on my credit account is —
c. generally about what I would expect
d. sometimes rather more than I'd expected

5. I usually first think about drinking —
a. when I wake up
b. some time during the morning
c. at lunchtime
d. late in the afternoon
e. in the evening

If you answered yes to a, b, or c, then also answer the following:

When I plan the rest of my day —
f. drinking is a high priority
g. drinking is not particularly important to me

6. *Before going to a social event —*
a. I never have a drink
b. I seldom have a drink
c. I usually have a drink

7. *When I decide whether to go to a social event —*
a. it doesn't matter to me whether or not alcohol is going to be available there
b. I prefer some drink to be available there
c. I don't really enjoy it unless some drink is going to be available
d. I will only attend if I know drink will be available there

8. *After I have had a few drinks —*
a. I never pretend to have had

less than I really have
b. I occasionally do pretend that
c. I often do pretend that
d. I sometimes declare I had one more drink than I've actually had

9. *When it gets towards closing time —*
a. I find I've had enough to drink
b. I tend to double my final order or buy some to take home with me

10. *In the course of everyday conversation my friends —*
a. seldom talk about drinking
b. quite often talk about drinking
If you answered yes to b, then also answer the following —
I have noticed that my friends usually —
c. joke about it
d. offer some kind of advice to me
e. talk about drinking much more than me

Add up your score as follows and then assess yourself according to the following 'categories':

1. a = 1, b = 1, c = 2, d = 3, e = 4
2. a = 1, b = 3, c = 2
3. a = 1, b = 1, c = 2, d = 3, e = 2, f = 1, g = 4, h = 2
4. a = 2, b = 1, c = 1, d = 2
5. a = 4, b = 3, c = 2, d = 1, e = 1, f = 3, g = 1

6. a = 1, b = 2, c = 3
7. a = 1, b = 2, c = 3, d = 4
8. a = 1, b = 3, c = 4, d = 2
9. a = 1, b = 3
10. a = 1, b = 2, c = 3, d = 4, e = 1

Relax: If you scored 17 or under you are not a dependent drinker and have no need to worry at present about your drinking habits. But don't forget that drinking habits can change, particularly in times of stress, and you may not *stay* a non-dependent drinker.

Be wary: If you scored from 18 to 24 you are likely to be a regular, but moderate drinker. You may feel a 'need' to drink now and then, and may be causing yourself harm — or causing others difficulties — from time to time.

You are in the area of mildly vulnerable drinking, and should watch your consumption carefully for signs of drinking more, or more often. If your friends say that you are starting to drink more, take heed: remember that it is easy to move along the continuum towards the problem end of drinking.

Cut down: If you scored 25 to 30, you are probably drinking regularly and drinking too much for the good of your health and relationships. You may not notice the 'need' to drink — because you are rarely going without it. You are now running a very high risk of developing more serious drink problems, so try to cut down the amount you drink, and to drink less often.

Seek help: If you scored over 31 you are probably dependent, physically and psychologically, on alcohol. You are certainly harming yourself and could be causing suffering to others.

If you stop drinking or try to cut down you may experience unpleasant withdrawal symptoms (trembling, sweating, feelings of panic), and may feel confused, moody or depressed. As time goes on you will need more and more alcohol to reach the same level of intoxication. You should seek help from one of the organisations listed at the end of this chapter.

STRATEGIES FOR CUTTING DOWN

Here are some suggestions to help you cut down your drinking, which can be adapted freely according to your taste or situation.

— Don't drink until a specific time in the day which you set for yourself, preferably to coincide with or to follow your evening meal.

— Don't drink at lunchtime. It will make you feel low in the afternoon as your blood sugar level sinks and the depressant effect follows the 'high'. You will probably feel tense as a result and feel the need to repeat the 'lift'. Sugary tea or food will raise your blood sugar level again — a better alternative to more alcohol.

— Alternate alcohol with soft drinks. This is a useful trick for parties or tense social situations when you feel nervous or under pressure.

— Don't allow your glass to be topped up until you have finished what is in it already. A lot of people keep drinking because they feel the need to do something with their hands in social situations, but there is a lot of comfort to be had from simply holding a glass.

— Arrange alternative activities in the times when you are in the habit of going to the pub. Relaxing activities like yoga or swimming will help you to unwind without alcohol. If you prefer more vigorous sports, beware the temptation to slake your thirst immediately afterwards with a few drinks. Drink fruit juice until you no longer feel thirsty.

— Make a pact with one or more friends that on given nights during the week you won't drink. Maybe you could meet and do something different with the money you have saved!

— Decide to stick to two non-drinking days a week — and tell people about your decision. Using the twenty units a week ceiling, this allows you four units on other days — which feels like a reasonable amount.

— Make a rule for yourself only to drink in company.

— Never drink more than two units of alcohol (a pint of beer, two glasses of wine) in one hour.

— Always order singles or half pints. The whole process of buying and drinking half pints takes twice as long as buying pints, and so your drink will seem to last longer.

— Make a list of the number of calories in each type of drink — and absorb the information. Then when you feel like another, think to yourself: would I now have another two pieces of toast (or the equivalent of about 200 calories)? The answer will probably be *no*, and the psychological deterrent effect will put you off that next drink.

— If you feel a craving for a drink, try satisfying it with a tasty morsel of food instead. You will be surprised at how often food can give you the lift you need.

PROFESSIONAL HELPING AGENCIES

If your drinking came into the 'seek help' category of the questionnaire above, you would be wise to contact a local treatment agency.

The best place to start is your local advice centre or citizen's advice bureau, which should be able to tell you about the services available in your area. Alternatively, look up your local Council on Alcoholism in the phone book. These are sometimes called Alcohol Problem Advisory Services, and there is a network of them across the country.

A good GP should, in theory, know about services, but all too often family doctors are ill-informed about alcohol problems. The social services and probation services also have some officers who should be able to advise you.

Unfortunately for women, the vast majority of facilities cater primarily to the needs of men although women are a third of the estimated three-quarters of a million problem drinkers in this country. FARE (the Federation of Alcoholism Rehabilitation Services) publishes a *Directory of Services*, which lists all facilities known to FARE in the UK. But this does *not* include women's groups or self-help groups, and of the services listed which say they take women, the ratio of men to women is generally very high.

WOMEN'S SPECIAL NEEDS

Women's needs in treatment are different from men's, but our needs are often overlooked. Women in mixed groups are generally at a disadvantage as drinking women are considered more 'deviant' and 'difficult' than men. Men in groups are also inclined to judge women harshly, and women's contributions may be cast aside as men hold the floor and women reproduce their usual pattern of listening.[7]

Women workers in DAWN and FARE have found that there is a 'myth of the aggressive woman drinker' which is related to the problem of homelessness.[8] Homelessness is often the main problem of women who start drinking after admission to hostels, but when women are offered decent accommodation their drinking usually decreases. So much do women drinkers dread the homeless state that they often stay in unsatisfactory relationships, or keep changing men, rather than stay in a hostel and become homeless.

As a result, homelessness for women drinkers is often a hidden problem. Workers in the alcohol field see so few homeless women that those they do see become more memorable. And, as homeless women, they are forced to compete for attention in male-dominated and male-oriented services, (only three women-only residential centres for alcoholic women exist in the UK) they are given a reputation for being aggressive.

Women also have special problems — beyond drinking — when they come to facilities for help. Many services lack creche facilities, so that mothers attending day centres have nowhere to leave their children. Residential treatment can provide a vital space for a woman to recuperate, but, again, her children are rarely taken into account. And there is the fear for the mother that if she seeks treatment her children will be taken into care and subsequently kept from her. (Advice centres and local Councils on Alcoholism can explain the legal side of this situation.)

There is the further problem of labelling for women. A lot of services for alcoholism are in psychiatric hospitals and so the women — already stigmatised by the title 'alcoholic' — is now also labelled 'psychiatric patient'.

SERVICES

Below is a brief run down of the type of services available in the UK. The FARE *Directory* is essentially a work of reference for professionals but it does give information about the programmes, treatment, philosophy and staffing of each service and agency, and also tells you about the admission procedures, transport to and from, and eligibility for the programme.

The Directory however, does not have the scope to evaluate these services in terms of their helpfulness to women, and services do vary enormously in style and quality. Nor does the *Directory* list women's groups or self-help groups.

Day centres: These have a wide range of functions. Some are information and counselling centres; they offer a variety of activities for both individuals and groups. Others deal with homeless alcoholics, referring them to hostels. They may be quite informal drop-in centres, or highly structured centres where you are required to attend regular activities.

Advice and counselling services (other than Councils on Alcoholism): These will provide advice and counselling and may be useful as a starting point to tackle a drinking problem.

Local Councils on Alcoholism (or Alcohol Problem Advisory Services): These vary greatly in size and emphasis, but generally local councils have a broad brief. They may coordinate local services, train non-specialist workers, run counselling services and groups, and offer social skills training.

Alcohol Treatment Units (ATUs): These are run by the NHS in hospitals, and you may be referred as a day-patient or an in-patient by your GP or social worker. (If you don't think your GP is well informed, go to an advice centre first to enquire about ATUs, and then ask your GP to refer you.)

ATUs have facilities for 'detoxification' (coming off drink), and help you to cope with withdrawal effects, often with the use of drugs. They generally provide counselling, group work and social skills training as well.

Residential facilities and hostels: These have living-in treatment pro-

rammes which may last from about six weeks to a year. They generally
un groups and give counselling. They may help with job-hunting at the
nd of treatment, or finding accommodation for the homeless.

sychiatric and General Hospitals: These may provide beds in their
vards for alcoholic patients on the same basis as ATUs. They may also
ake day-patients, and provide groups and counselling. Your GP will
efer you for treatment.

rivate facilities: These are usually residential and vastly expensive (from
200 to £800 a week). They don't provide much more than the other
acilities — except a richer class of problem drinker.

M Services facilities: These exist for people in the armed forces, but
ome do take local people as well.

THER GROUPS

---

rinkwatchers: This is a 'club' not intended for 'alcoholics' who need to
bstain, but for those whose lifestyle involves alcohol, or alcohol mis-
sers who want to cut down. Drinkwatchers say that it is 'okay to drink
- but important to drink sensibly'. They meet each week for about two
ours and then socialise in local pubs or wine bars to practise their new
kills.

Like ACCEPT, the day centre which is partly responsible for its pro-
ramme, Drinkwatchers is inclined to attract fairly 'upmarket' people
ho are comfortable with their therapies.

Their aim is to learn to relax, to learn to say 'no' to drinks, to be aware
 drinking patterns, to cope with difficult situations without alcohol, and
 develop a healthier way of life.

There are now three groups in London and various others are being set
p across the country. Each group has about a dozen members. As yet
ere is not a women-only group. Contact Drinkwatchers through
CCEPT on 01-381 3155.

lcoholics Anonymous: AA is a world-wide network of mutual aid, sup-
ort and self-help groups which now has over a million members. There
 no doubt that it has been enormously effective in helping huge
umbers of alcoholics to give up alcohol, and has saved innumerable lives
 the process. However, the style and ideology of AA is not to everyone's
ste.

AA group meetings take two basic forms. At open meetings, which anyone may attend, there is usually a chairperson and a speaker, and alcoholics in the group will talk about their experiences. Closed meetings are for AA members only, to enable alcoholics to discuss their problems amongst themselves.

The only requirement for AA membership is the desire to stop drinking, and there are no dues or membership fees. AA stays strictly non aligned and non-sectarian.

The aim of members is to stay sober and to help others 'achieve sobriety'. The question of 'what is alcoholism?' is rarely discussed at AA where the emphasis is on recovery from, rather than investigation into the causes of alcohol problems.

The structure of the organisation is non-hierarchical, with power lying in the groups rather than at the centre. Typically, AA's central body is called, *not* the Board of Directors, but the General Service Board.

AA uses very simple, gospel-type formulae, like the 'Twelve Traditions', the 'Three Legacies' and the 'Twelve Steps'. The latter, for instance, are steps intended to direct alcoholics along the road to recovery and 'spiritual growth'. The First Step is to admit 'we were powerless over alcohol'. The Second Step is 'to believe that a Power greater than ourselves could restore us to sanity'. The other Steps encourage the practice of self-criticism, confession and reparation of past wrongs, surrender to 'God's will ('as we understand *Him*' (my italics)), prayer and meditation and carrying the message to other alcoholics.

AA claims to use spiritual rather than religious methods, but this process of moving from despair through confession to penance, hope and faith follows the pattern of various religious practices. AA members commonly talk in terms of 'conversion' to their new life.

These methods do work for many alcoholics who come to AA in a desperate, fearful and confused state. There is, however, a tendency to encourage people to survive by accepting their given circumstances and learning 'humility'. In its policy of avoiding all controversy, AA is not concerned with causes of problems or with working for social change.

And the organisation itself — rather than alcohol — can become the structure on which the recovering alcoholic depends. 'I used to go to the pub everyday; now I go to meetings everyday,' said one member at an open meeting.

AA is resistant to the idea of women-only groups — and to any form of group that changes the criterion for membership from the simple 'desire to stop drinking'. However, a few women-only groups have been attempted in AA, but have not survived.

And although its female membership has grown enormously to the present ratio of one woman to every three men, it remains essentially male oriented. The AA 'bible', *Alcoholics Anonymous*, includes a chapter called 'To Wives', but there isn't one addressed to husbands.

The groups do vary widely in character according to location and luck, and, for many drinkers with severe problems, it is the best available solution. Local groups are often listed in telephone directories, or contact the national office at 11 Redcliffe Gardens, London SW10 (01-352 9779). AA also have family support groups called Al-Anon, and Al-Ateen for younger drinkers.

The four national charities: Other groups involved in education and information, and in coordinating alcoholism services, are the NCA (National Council on Alcoholism), the AEC (Alcohol Education Centre), the MCA (Medical Council on Alcoholism) and FARE (Federation of Alcoholism Rehabilitation Establishments). These, however, are on the verge of reorganisation.

DAWN (Drugs, Alcohol and Women — Nationally) is a pressure group working for better understanding and treatment of drug and alcohol problems in women. Contact DAWN through the London Council on Alcoholism, 146 Queen Victoria Street, London EC4.

Coping with a drinker in the family: In this book I have focused on alcohol's effects on women *as drinkers*, but of course we are also vastly affected by other people's drinking problems, especially within a family unit. Alcoholism is often called 'the family illness', and much of the literature suggests that marital conflict, poor parent-child relationships, social isolation and communication problems are characteristic of families of both men and women with drinking problems.[9]

If you are living with a problem drinker, you are likely to need help and support yourself. Some services, such as ACCEPT, have relatives groups, or contact Al-Anon family groups at 61 Great Dover Street, London SE1 Tel: 01-403 0888.

WORKERS IN THE ALCOHOL FIELD:
THREE ALTERNATIVES IN TREATMENT

A DAY CENTRE

Women's groups for drinkers are still rare, but centres like ACCEPT (Alcohol Community Centres for Education, Prevention and Treatment) do run women's groups as part of their treatment programme.

ACCEPT in Fulham is one of England's largest alcoholism clinics and it is unusual for its high proportion (nearly half) of women clients. The clinic's director, Charles Vetter, thinks this is a reflection of sexism in the conventional treatment field:

> Male treatment systems, male literature (i.e. a book entitled *So Your Husband Has a Drinking Problem* and no booklet *So Your Wife Has a Drinking Problem*), male doctors and consultants, males in the past having greatly outnumbered females in treatment, all these factors have led to male chauvinism in the alcohol field and the theory that women are more difficult to treat than men.
>
> Perhaps women are more difficult to treat than men, but they deserve an equal opportunity in treatment. We use a high propor-tion of women as counsellors — which in turn attracts women as clients.

Most of these clients have been triggered into drinking heavily by events in their lives which have left them with feelings of loss — such as a death in the family, a broken marriage or romance, or children leaving home:

> We have one client who was a 'social drinker' for fifty years. Then her sister died, she suffered a lot of stress, and within three months she was drinking two to four bottles of sherry a day.
>
> Most women begin drinking in the first place as a consequence of social pressure. When a woman goes out on a date with a man she doesn't want to be 'square', and finds it very difficult to say — no thank you. A woman doctor recently told me that she had to stop drinking while taking some tablets, but other people

continued to try to force drink on her.

Men often think that pressurising a woman to drink is a good way to lower her sexual defences. I used to be a world champion male chauvinist pig[1] and when I wanted to get a woman to bed I would buy her a lot of drink in the hope that it would make her more amenable.

For women the consequences of such tactics can lead to enormous guilt and shame — and unwanted pregnancy. One Birmingham birth-control clinic has found that of the women who asked for the morning-after pill, a high proportion reported drinking heavily.

Men tend to start drinking for different reasons from women: this is Charles' explanation:

Men's drinking is part of the manhood ritual of growing up. Then it is a question of drink sneaking up on them. Men are more inclined to feel stress as the result of their jobs. For instance, a man who gets promoted may feel under a lot of pressure which he then tries to relieve with drink.

Women are conditioned to look for different things in life from men, and are trained into being household slaves, mothers and cooks.

Most women don't have any choice. They are trapped. Women are supposed to get their jollies through others — which can lead to feelings of emptiness and depression.

And deferring to males is a very powerful syndrome. By not asserting themselves, women lose their self esteem, they feel resentments and emotional discomforts. One way to relieve this is with alcohol.

Vetter is fond of referring to what he calls the Used Car Syndrome, in which a husband treats his drinking wife as if she was his car:

He expects daily, reliable service from her including her work as a household slave, as child minder, cook and sexual object.

When she 'breaks down' (i.e. starts drinking heavily) and neglects her chores, he will bring her in for 'repairs'. He will diligently resist any self-examination or counselling to develop insight into his role in creating marriage problems.

This is not at all unusual behaviour on the part of husbands. I had one man who brought his wife in and reeled off a list of complaints: she wasn't doing this, she wasn't doing that, the dinner wasn't ready, the house wasn't clean. He read me his Bill of Indictment and said — I'm leaving her here with you.

After she'd been through treatment, she went home, and it was only a few weeks before she again 'broke down'. The husband rang me up and indignantly told me, 'You haven't done her a bit of good' — implying that his 'used car' is unreliable and that the 'garage' (the treatment agency) is guilty of poor workmanship.

In certain cases, after repeated breakdowns, and when the husband can afford it, he will trade in his 'used car', his wife, for a new model.

And leaving their spouse because of drinking is something husbands are far more likely to do than wives, largely because men tend to have more economic freedom than women:

Men can move to a new town, get a new job, find a new partner more easily than women. And an older man can find a younger woman more easily than an older woman can find a new husband.

Women also tend to be more caring and loyal. They are trained from childhood to protect the family — and so often protect their drinking husband — which makes the situation worse.

In the ACCEPT relatives' group, (for relatives to learn how best to help the drinker in their family), women outnumber men by ten to one.

A counsellor's experience: Jean Clack has worked as a counsellor at ACCEPT since 1979. She finds little difference, except in degree, between the underlying problems of women who have resorted to drink, and the problems of women in general.

Jean has never had a drink problem, but as she trained to become a counsellor she became aware of the other difficulties which hampered her as a woman — and which she now regularly encounters in her clients:

At forty-one I went through a 'middle-age crisis'. I didn't know what I was doing with my life. I had been at home for so many years before I started work at ACCEPT that my self-esteem was very low. I did have a job in the City when I was younger, but by the time I was forty I had come to believe that I would never be able to work again. The ACCEPT programme of assertiveness-training and group therapy helped me to recognise that I still had an opportunity to do something which interested me.

I find that the women who come to the clinic often have the same difficulties that I had myself — low self-esteem, oppressive conditioning and the man-woman thing.

Jean commonly sees women who are experiencing conflicts between their personal needs, and the behaviour expected of them in the traditional roles of wife or mother or lover:

I can't come in this evening as I've got to be home to get Johnny's tea' — that's the kind of thing they tell me. Then I discover that Johnny is sixteen. 'But I've always done it,' they say. I tell them it might do Johnny some good to take care of his mother for a change.

As women do become more assertive in the course of the ACCEPT programme, their husbands are inclined to feel threatened:

The husbands feel fear when they find they've got a new person on their hands. We encourage relatives of clients to attend the relatives' groups — and husbands tend to get angry during the sessions. Sometimes the relationship breaks down altogether, which, in some cases, is appropriate.

Other women clients have worries about domestic duties:

Either they are having trouble keeping up with the housework, or they are so obsessed with doing housework that they have to face the terrible problem of — what next? — when it gets to eleven o'clock.

Jean believes that women can only tackle these problems when we grasp hold of the idea that we have our own rights as individuals. Some women who go to the clinic say that they are motivated to attend by other people. One of Jean's clients began the programme saying she was doing it for her son. But after a while she was saying, 'Sod it, I'm doing it for *me.*'

Jean is not anti-drinking per se. But she does believe that women who have been drinking in order to release inhibitions and express their emotions can learn to do this without risking dependency on alcohol:

You can learn to get these feelings going, express these pent-up emotions — like anger — without drink. If you release them while drinking no one takes much notice anyway.

Jean's observations are borne out by these comments, written in note form after an art class by one of ACCEPT's woman clients:

From the cradle to the grave society is concerned with jobs, incomes, mortgages, politics etc. Individuals continue on a dull treadmill with little opportunity to discover that they can develop an inner life of their own. (Hence also maimed personalities.)

It is often difficult to communicate and 'dig out' problems through words ... many people cannot express emotions in words. Sometimes it must be easier for them to express their feelings with their hands — especially if they feel they are being left to do their own thing.

Whatever is stored inside us rots. Whatever comes out can be put to advantage — as can be seen from a very beautiful and sensitive drawing made by a man whose hand was shaking so much that he could not hold a coffee cup.

(These notes, written to Charles Vetter, end with an apologetic and self-deprecatory postscript: 'Charles, these are only notes. I am not too sure what you wanted. I do not wish to teach my grandmother how to suck eggs.')

And what happens to women's lives *after* going through the ACCEPT programme? Jean reflects on her own experience:

Many women make big changes. Some go back to work after being at home for years. Look at me for instance. I changed roles completely and now I'm doing a full-time job. My family felt very threatened at first. One of my children (who took a year and a half to tell me) eventually said — I'm glad now that you went back to work. You're not so moody and I don't feel I've done everything wrong all the time.

A RESIDENTIAL HOUSE

Whereas day centres like ACCEPT are appropriate to the needs of problem drinkers who still have a home to go to, others who have lost their homes need a different kind of support.

Fiona Richmond is a social worker for London's Alcoholics Recovery Project (ARP). She runs a mixed residential house.[2]

She has worked with many women, each of whom has had problems particular to their individual circumstances. But she has found that there are broad patterns of drinking amongst women, which are related to our social position and the pressures on women. In simplified terms she characterises her clients' problems like this:

Some women who go the traditional way of marriage and children find that it doesn't make them happy. They feel unsatisfied, unfulfilled or feel the demands upon them are too great.

One of my clients who married very young always felt she had to live up to the high expectations of her husband. He had rigid ideas about how his children should be brought up, how the house should be perfectly kept, etc.

He was a farmer and she shared much of his work, doing the accounts and entertaining farm reps when they came to visit. Yet this woman never felt she was good enough. And so she drank to give her the confidence to act the role which was expected of her.

Another of Fiona's clients had a life that was miserable by any standards. After early marriage and early divorce she worked very hard in Scotland to bring up her child alone:

For thirty years her life was a drudge. She drank for energy to get on with things at the end of the day, and to seek oblivion from her life. She felt at the same time resentful that she was being forced into living up to being a 'good mother' — and a 'failure', as she felt that this wasn't really the case. 'I *should* have been able to do it,' is how she puts it now. She is a victim of imposed pressure from the expectations of society.

Then there is the woman who doesn't get married and who doesn't have children. Her feeling is 'there's something wrong with me'. She might be very successful in her work (one of Fiona's clients who felt this was qualified and employed as a nurse) but underneath she feels worthless. The conflict between what is expected of her and what she *feels* is such that she 'needs' alcohol to blot it out.

And in recent years Fiona has noticed a considerable increase in the number of young women needing treatment who have been drinking since their early teens. Sometimes these women are suffering from unmet emotional needs.

One of Fiona's clients started life with rejection by her own mother, went on to a psychiatric locked institution at the age of eight, and grew up without love, without security and without skills. By the age of twenty she had made numerous suicide attempts, and had had a child which was subsequently taken from her. 'It is hard to know how to help her,' says Fiona. 'She drinks to escape the reality of what her life is like, and for comfort.'

As severe as the problems of her clients are, Fiona believes their experiences are relevant to other women drinkers. Their problems are not unique to a separate breed of persons called 'alcoholics'. She sees them as existing at the extreme end of a common line of experience:

The difference between 'alcoholics' and other drinkers is one of the level of drinking and the degree of problems which follow. The women I work with talk about 'how it was five years ago and how it could be again'. Most of them believe that if circumstances had been different, things would have been okay.

Fiona leads the group meetings in which the women are encouraged to talk about their feelings and to learn to communicate again without alcohol. In these meetings, sexuality emerges as a big issue: These women are victims of strong stereotypes about what women should be. Feminine identity is hard enough to establish for any woman, but the 'unfeminine' problem of being a drinker aggravates the situation. They feel it is bad enough to be a drinker — but extra-bad because you are a woman.

Women receive many 'messages' from society about what they 'are' or what they 'should be' as women. My clients talk about the extremes of being a woman: either you are meant to be perfect, giving, loving and all-caring. Or, at the other extreme, you are a whore and a slut. They talk about wanting to be the first kind of ideal woman — but feeling like the second. They say — 'I'm only a slut.'

In Fiona's experience there are essential differences between women and men when it comes to drinking — and some important parallels:

Men will put their drinking down to environmental causes. They will say — it was my job. Or — we all did it. Or sometimes it is emotional, for instance — when my wife left me.

But women usually put their drinking down to emotional needs. They are inclined to suffer from a sense of inadequacy, depression and lack of confidence.

Another important difference is that men drink in public but women do it privately. My women clients talk about drinking behind locked doors, closing the windows and curtains — just me and the bottle.

Where men and women are *alike*, is that both sexes will drink when what is expected of them doesn't fit with what they are:

The vulnerable man who feels he should be macho may drink to ease the strain. It is a political issue: the ways in which society defines us does damage to both sexes.

A WOMEN'S GROUP

Ann Hall is a social worker who, after years of experience in the alcohol field,[3] saw that the needs of her women clients were not being met by any of the existing facilities. Drawing on the lessons of the women's movement about the value of supportive, consciousness-raising, women-only groups, she decided (together with her colleague Jo Cleary), to set up such a group for women problem drinkers.

The women in this group, aged from twenty-five to thirty-five, had all experienced severe problems as a consequence of their drinking. Some had been in trouble with the law, and one woman had lost her eyesight as the result of a fight. Yet most had paid jobs — some were secretaries, some were teachers — and were coping well with other aspects of their lives.

The specific reasons why people drink are as individual as the person, but as the women in this group discussed their common experiences, a pattern began to emerge which Ann describes:

> We found that the preoccupations of the drinkers in our group were very much of the kind that feminists identify as women's problems — difficulties with relationships, lack of assertiveness, the inability to express anger, and the loneliness and depression which stems from being stuck at home.
>
> From the beginning we decided that the group was there not to talk about drinking as such, but to look at what was behind the drinking and to discover the million other underlying problems. What we found was the desire to forget, to blot out, to not cope, to do things without being responsible and without remembering. And the desire to be 'me' — without being hurt.
>
> Anxiety was also a major factor. The women would describe themselves as feeling generally strung up. Whether this was a cause or a result of drinking I don't know. We had many unresolved arguments about it. For most of them their anxiety was a panic about the effort of living, the feeling that I don't fit into all this, that I'm not very good at anything, that I'm inferior. That I don't like recognising my needs for other people. That I don't like being vulnerable.

Acceptance of self was a fundamental problem for the women in the group:

> Many of them were trying to come to terms with who they were and what they wanted. Many of the women also found it difficult to recognise and express their sexual needs. The permission thing came out very strongly — the feeling that I *shouldn't* be like this.
>
> They felt — other people don't like me, I've got nothing to offer, I'm worthless. They felt — I've not done what I'm supposed to do, i.e. get a man, have kids.
>
> But most of the women didn't really want this anyway. What they *did* want was to be valued, loved, respected, to be interesting, to be able to cope on their own. What they needed was confidence, assertiveness, belief in self, a sense of their own value.
>
> Jo and I decided early on that we were not going to make any

kind of condemnation of drinking behaviour in the group. And then on one occasion most of the group got together socially and went on a massive bender. They all got very drunk, continued drinking at a night club, got themselves into trouble and were nearly arrested.

At the next group meeting after this drinking bout we made no comment about the incident. The women reacted with anger. They wanted us to collude in their guilt by telling them they were wrong for doing it. They wanted us to take the responsibility. We didn't, and it was a turning point in the group. The women started to take responsibility for themselves.

Many of the techniques of psychotherapy were used to explore the group's legacy of unexplored feelings. Ann was struck by the women's inability to express anger:

Most of them had had pretty bad experiences, with their parents for instance, but had never expressed any anger.

One woman in the group had a schizophrenic father and brother, and she was carrying the whole weight of that family at the age of twenty-two. She would drink and drink and drink to escape. She was caring for all the others at the expense of herself. We wanted her to get angry and to start saying, I'm important, but we never quite achieved it.

On one occasion another woman in the group *did* get angry for the first time and she started shouting that she hated her family. All the tensions in the group exploded at once.

We realised after that that a lot of the women had never been able to say that they needed things. They had always felt guilty about wanting things, about making demands, about saying that their feelings mattered. Some of them were saying, I'm important, for the first time ever.

Ann believes that the group itself not only provided its own tools for discovering the problems behind drinking, but that it helped the women to support each other in very positive and practical ways. Eventually the women came to see that it was possible for them to make important changes in their lives — a vital realisation for women whose choices are restricted on all sides:

Housing, family, restraints and money were problems for most of them. These social and political issues are inseparable from women's drinking.

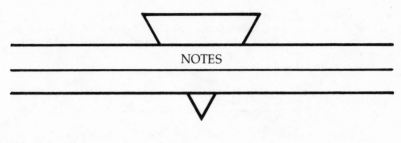

NOTES

INTRODUCTION

1. R.G.Ferrence, 'Sex Differences in the Prevalence of Problem Drinking' in *Alcohol and Drug Problems in Women*, O.J. Kalant (ed.), Plenum Press, 1980.
2. Conclusions gathered by a meeting of the Alcohol Counselling Service, 34 Electric Lane, London SW9, on drinking and the ethnic minorities, August 1982.

Chapter 2: SOCIAL DRINKING

1. That 'social' drinkers give many of the same reasons for drinking as 'problem' drinkers do is further confirmation that there is no clear divide between the two types of drinking pattern. See chapter 6 for discussion of terms.
2. Bill Saunders, 'Psychological Aspects of Women and Alcohol', in *Woman and Alcohol*, Camberwell Council on Alcoholism, Tavistock, 1980.
3. *Ibid.*
4. Dight, S.E., *Scottish Drinking Habits*, London HMSO, 1976.
5. Equal Opportunities Commission, Overseas House, Quay Street, Manchester M3 3HN; Tel: 061 833 9244. The EOC publish a pamphlet on sex discrimination on licensed premises called 'Time Ladies and Gentlemen Please'.

Chapter 3: A WOMAN'S PLACE

1. Brovermann, I.K., Brovermann, D.M. *et al.*, 'Sex Role Stereotyping and Clinical Judgements of Mental Health,' *Journal of Consulting and Clinical Psychology*, Vol. 34, Part 1, pages 1-7, 1970.
2. Bridget Hutter and Gillian Williams, 'Controlling Women: The Normal and the Deviant' in *Controlling Women*, Croom Helm, 1981.
3. Shirley Otto, 'Women, Alcohol and Social Control' in *Controlling Women, op. cit.*
4. Nancy Milford, *Zelda Fitzgerald*, Bodley Head, 1970.
5. Junius Adams and Michael Leitch, *Alcohol*, Omnibus Press, 1978.
6. Shirley Otto, *op. cit.*
7. Report from First DAWN Symposium, 28 November, 1980. From London Council on Alcoholism, 146 Queen Victoria Street, London EC4.
8. Shirley Otto, *op. cit.*
9. Helping Hand Organisation, 'Female Alcoholics', 1976.

10. The *Guardian*, 17 September 1982.

11. Jean Kinney and Gwen Leaton, *Loosening the Grip*, C.V.Mosby, St Louis, 1978.

12. Avon Council on Alcoholism, 'A Survey of Gateways to Treatment for Women in Avon 1982', Avon Council on Alcoholism, 14 Park Row, Bristol.

13. Hutter and Williams, *op. cit.*

Chapter 4: THE POLITICS OF ALCOHOL

1. 'Alcohol Policies in the UK', Report by the Central Policy Review Staff, May 1979. Published by Sociologiska Institutionem, Stockholm Universitet, S106 91, Stockholm, Sweden, April 1982.

2. *About Women and Alcohol*, Scriptographic Publications Ltd, 1982. Available from National Council on Alcoholism, 3 Grosvenor Crescent, London SW1.

3. FARE Newsletter Aug/Sept 1982. Women and Alcohol, Statistics.

4. *Ibid.*

5. Stan Shaw, 'The Causes of Increasing Drinking Problems Amongst Women' in *Women and Alcohol*, Camberwell Council on Alcoholism, Tavistock, 1980.

6. 'Alcoholics Anonymous, Survey of Alcoholics Anonymous in Great Britain', Report from General Service Board of AA, Great Britain Ltd, 1981. Available from Alcoholics Anonymous, 11 Redcliffe Gardens, London SW10.

7. Stan Shaw, *op. cit.*

8. *Ibid.*

9. National Institute on Alcohol Abuse and Alcoholism, *Women and Alcohol*, May 1980. National Clearinghouse For Alcohol Information, PO Box 2345, Rockville, Maryland, 20852, USA.

10. *Ibid.*

11. Stan Shaw, *op. cit.*

12. R.E. Kendell, 'Alcoholism: A Medical or a Political Problem?' *British Medical Journal*, 10 February 1979.

13. Stan Shaw, *op. cit.*

14. Office of Health Economics, 'Alcohol, Reducing the Harm', April 1981 Available from 12 Whitehall, London SW1.

15. Stan Shaw, *op. cit.*

16. R.E. Kendell, *op. cit.*

17. 'Alcohol, Reducing the Harm', *op. cit.*

18. *Ibid.*

19. Ledermann S. *Alcool, Alcoolisme, Alcoolisation*, Paris, Presses Universitaires de France, 1956.

20. R.E Kendell, *op. cit.*

21. *Ibid.*

22. Richard Smith, 'Alcohol and Alcoholism: The Politics of Alcohol', *British Medical Journal*, 8 May 1982.

23. 'Alcohol Policies in the UK', *op. cit.*

24. *Ibid.*

25. House of Commons Expenditure Committee (1977), 'Report on Preventive Medicine', vols. 1-3, HMSO, London. See also Royal College of Psychiatrists (1979), 'Alcohol and Alcoholism', Tavistock; Advisory Committee on Alcoholism (1978), 'Report on Prevention', DHSS and Welsh Office: London; World Health

Organization (1980), 'Problems Related to Alcohol Consumption', Technical Report Series No. 650, WHO, Geneva.

26. 'Alcohol Policies in the UK', *op. cit.*

27. 'Cirrhosis as a Growth Investment Opportunity?' editorial in *British Journal of Addiction*, 77, 1982.

28. DHSS, 'Drinking Sensibly', HMSO, 1981.

29. Richard Smith, *op. cit.*

30. *Ibid.*

31. *Ibid.*

32. *Labour Research*, 1980. No. 69, page 173.

33. *Labour Research, op. cit.*, pages 170-172.

34. 'Alcohol, Reducing the Harm', *op. cit.*

35. Richard Smith, *op. cit.*

36. Mike Daube, 'Disorderly House' in *Times Health Supplement*, 25 December 1981.

37. *Ibid.*

38. *Ibid.*

39. *Ibid.*

40. Richard Smith, *op. cit.*

41. Mike Daube, *op. cit.*

42. DHSS and NCVO, 'National Voluntary Organizations and Alcohol Misuse', September 1982.

43. 'Alcohol Policies in the UK', *op. cit.*

44. *Ibid.*

45. 'Cirrhosis as a Growth Investment Opportunity', *op. cit.*

46. *Ibid.*

Chapter 5: BAD NEWS FOR WOMEN DRINKERS

1. Office of Health Economics, 'Alcohol: Reducing the Harm', April 1981.

2. Avon Council on Alcoholism, 'Women and Alcohol: A Survey of Gateways to Treatment for Women in Avon, 1982', Avon Council on Alcoholism.

3. Dr. H.D. Chalke, 'Man's Alcoholic Equal?' *British Journal on Alcohol and Alcoholism*, Vol 16.2, 1981.

4. Camberwell Council on Alcoholism, .*Women and Alcohol*, Tavistock, 1980.

5. Avon Council on Alcoholism, *op. cit.*

6. Stuart Kuttner and Neil Blincow, 'Postal Parson's £100,000 Mission' in *Evening Standard*, 26 April 1977.

7. Maxine Feifer, 'Don't Start Your Baby on the Drink', *Forum*, vol. 12, no. 2.

Chapter 6: ABOUT ALCOHOL

1. Chafetz and Demone, 'Alcoholism and Society', OUP, New York, 1962.

2. National Council on Alcoholism, 'What Everyone Should Know about Alcohol', Scriptographic Publications, 1981.

3. Office of Health Economics, 'Alcohol: Reducing the Harm', April 1981.

4. J.Adams and M.Leitch, *Alcohol*, Omnibus Press, 1978.

5. National Council on Alcoholism, *op. cit.*

6. Office of Health Economics, *op. cit.*

7. Health Education Council, 'Facts About Alcohol', HEC, 78 New Oxford Street, London WC1.

8. J.Adams and M.Leitch, *op. cit.*

9. *Ibid.*

10. *Ibid.*

Chapter 7: ALCOHOL IN YOUR BODY

1. *PMT, The Unrecognized Illness,* Judy Lever with the help of Dr M. Brush and B. Haynes, Melbourne House, London, 1979.

2. *Ibid.*

3. Office of Health Economics, 'Alcohol: Reducing the Harm', April 1981.

4. British Medical Bulletin, 'Alcohol and Disease', 1982. Vol. 38, Churchill Livingstone.

Chapter 8: ALCOHOL AND PREGNANCY

1. National Council of Women, 'Alcohol and the Unborn Child: The Foetal Alcohol Syndrome', March 1980, National Council of Women, 36 Lower Sloane Street, London SW1.

2. *Ibid.*

3. Ann Streissguth, Sharon Landesmann-Dwyer, Joan C. Martin, David Smith, 'Teratogenic Effects of Alcohol in Humans and Laboratory Animals', *Science,* vol. 209, 18 July 1980.

4. P. Lemoine *et al., Ouest Med.* 25, 477, 1968. (English translation available from National Clearinghouse for Alcohol Information, Department STIAR, PO Box 2345, Rockville, Maryland 20852, USA.)

5. Kenneth Jones, David Smith *et al.,* 'Pattern of Malformation in Offspring of Chronic Alcoholic Mothers', *The Lancet,* 9 June 1973.

6. Ann Streissguth, *op. cit.*

7. National Council of Women, *op. cit.*

8. *Ibid.*

9. Ann Streissguth, *op. cit.*

10. Ann Streissguth, a lecture, reported in *New Scientist,* 11 January 1979.

11. Pamela Dowdell, 'Alcohol and Pregnancy, A Review of the Literature 1968-80', *Nursing Times,* 21 October 1981.

12. Information and Feature Service, 'Women and Alcohol', August 1979, National Clearinghouse for Alcohol Information.

13. Royal College of Psychiatrists, 'Addendum to Alcohol and Alcoholism', Tavistock, 1979.

14. David Smith, 'Alcohol Effects on the Fetus, Fetal Drug Syndrome', *American Academy of Pediatrics,* 1979.

15. National Council of Women, *op. cit.*

16. Ruth Little, 'Drinking During Pregnancy: Implications for Public Health', Alcohol Health and Research World, Fall 1979.

17. National Council of Women, *op. cit.*

18. *Ibid.*

19. *Ibid.*

20. Ruth Little, 'Open Letter to *The Caring Community*', 364 High Road, Willesden, London NW10.

21. National Council of Women, *op. cit.*

22. *Ibid.*

23. Alison Macfarlane, 'Saving Money: Spending Lives', *Medicine in Society*, vol. 8, no. 1.

24. J.W.T. Dickerson, S. Baker, B. Barnes, 'Environmental Factors and Foetal Health — The Case for Pre-Conceptual Care'. Foresight, Woodhurst, Hydestile, Godalming, Surrey GU8 4AY.

25. *Ibid.*

Chapter 9: HANGOVERS: 'THE WRATH OF GRAPES'

1. David Outerbridge, *The Hangover Handbook*, Pan, 1981.

2. *Ibid.*

3. Robert Linn, *You Can Drink and Stay Healthy*, Sphere, 1981.

4. David Outerbridge, *op. cit.*

Chapter 10: DO YOU HAVE A DRINKING PROBLEM?

1. A. Paton and J.B. Saunders, *British Medical Journal*, 7 November 1981.

2. Griffith Edwards, *The Treatment of Drinking Problems*, Grant and McIntyre, 1982.

3. Office of Health Economics, 'Alcohol: Reducing the Harm', 1981.

4. Max Glatt, *Alcoholism*, Hodder and Stoughton, 1982.

5. Office of Health Economics, *op. cit.*

6. *Ibid.*

7. DAWN and FARE Joint Conference Notes, 1982.

8. *Ibid.*

9. Clare Wilson, 'The Family, Women and Alcohol' in *Women and Alcohol*, Camberwell Council on Alcoholism, Tavistock, 1980.

Chapter 11: WORKERS IN THE ALCOHOL FIELD: THREE ALTERNATIVES IN TREATMENT

1. Vetter's 'non-sexist' self-image and pronouncements on male chauvinism need to be taken with a pinch of salt. His personality dominates the clinic, and in our interview he literally talked down to me (seated on a low chair) from his large desk, his back to the light. On one occasion when I arrived in the clinic with a hangover I felt uncomfortable with the 'assertiveness' of the staff, and my personal feeling was that if I had gone there in a low state for help with drinking problems, I would have felt quite unnerved. On the other hand, there is no doubt that this clinic is dynamic and forward-looking, and has helped many people.

2. Although Fiona is committed to the idea of a one-to-one gender ratio in the

house, such is the shame and guilt felt by women alcoholics that they are reticent about coming forward and there are usually fewer women than men living in the house.

3. Ann started working in the alcohol field at the Alcoholics Recovery Project (ARP) in London in 1973. She subsequently ran a hostel for drinkers in Leicester between 1976 and 1979, and then worked for Camden Alcoholic Support Association (CASA) from 1979 to 1981, during which time she organised the women's group. She now works in the Single Homeless Project.

USEFUL ADDRESSES

Al-Anon Family Group Headquarters
P.O. Box 182
Madison Square Station
New York, New York   10159
  212/683-1771

Alateen (same as above)

ADPA
Alcohol and Drug Problems Association
  of North America, Inc.
444 North Capitol Street, N.W.
Washington, D.C.   20001
  202/737-4340

A.A.
Alcoholics Anonymous
General Service Office
P.O. Box 459
Grand Central Station
New York, New York   10163
  212/686-1100

American Council on Alcohol Problems, Inc.
2908 Patricia Dr.
Des Moines, Iowa   50322
  515/276-7752

American Council for Drug Education
6193 Executive Boulevard
Rockville, Maryland   20852
(formerly: American Council on Marijuana & c.)
  301/984-5700

AMSA
American Medical Society on Alcoholism
12 West 21st Street, 7th floor
New York, New York   10010
  212/206-6770

AHHAP
Association of Halfway House Alcoholism
  Programs of North America
786 East 7th Street
St. Paul, Minnesota   55106
  612/771-0933

ALMACA
Association of Labor-Management Administrators
  and Consultants on Alcoholism, Inc.
1800 N. Kent Street
Arlington, Virginia   22209
  703/522-6272

CSPI
Center for Science in the Public Interest
1501 16th Street, N.W.
Washington, D.C.   20036
  202/332-9110

COAF
Children of Alcoholics Foundation, Inc.
540 Madison Avenue, 23rd floor
New York, New York   10022
  212/980-5860

Citizen's Council on Women, Alcohol and Drugs
8293 Main Street
Ellicott City, Maryland   21043

Hazelden Foundation
Box 11
Center City, Minnesota   55012
  800/328-9000

ICAA/American
International Council on Alcohol and Addiction /
  American Foundation
P.O. Box 489
Locust Valley, New York   11560
  516/676-1802

The Johnson Institute
10700 Olson Memorial Highway
Minneapolis, Minnesota   55441-6199
  612/544-4165

MADD
Mothers Against Drunk Driving
669 Airport Freeway, Suite 310
Hurst, Texas   76053
  817/268-6233

Multi-Cultural Prevention Work Group
c/o Annette Green
Allegheny County MHMR/DA Program
429 Forbest Avenue, 9th floor
Pittsburgh, Pennsylvania   15219
(substance abuse among Native
Americans, other minorities)
  412/355-4291

NADAC
National Association of Alcoholism
  and Drug Abuse Counselors, Inc.
951 South George Mason Drive, Suite 204
Arlington, Virginia   22204
  703/920-4644

NAATP
National Association of Alcoholism Treatment
 Programs, Inc.
2082 Michelson Drive
Irvine, California 92715
 714/975-0104

NACOA
National Association of Children of Alcoholics, Inc.
P.O. Box 421691
San Francisco, California 94142
 415/431-1366

NAGAP
National Association of Gay Alcoholism
 Professionals, Inc.
204 West 20th Street
New York, New York 10011
 212/807-0634

NASADAD
National Association of State Alcohol and Drug
 Abuse Directors, Inc.
444 North Capitol Street, N.W.
Washington, D.C. 20001
 202/783-6868

NBAC
National Black Alcoholism Council
310 S. Michigan Avenue, Suite 1804
Chicago, Illinois 60604
 312/341-9466

NCALI
National Clearinghouse for Alcohol Information
P.O. Box 2345
Rockville, Maryland 20852
 301/468-2600

NCA
National Council on Alcoholism, Inc.
12 West 21st Street, 7th floor
New York, New York 10010
 212/206-6770

NCA/Public Policy
National Council on Alcoholism
 Office of Public Policy
1511 K Street, N.W., Suite 320
Washington, D.C. 20005
 202/737-8122

NIAAA
National Institute on Alcohol Abuse and Alcoholism
Parklawn Building
5600 Fishers Lane
Rockville, Maryland 20852
 301/443-3885

NIDA
National Institute on Drug Abuse
Parklawn Building
5600 Fishers Lane
Rockville, Maryland 20852
 301/443-4577

NNSA
National Nurses Society on Addiction
2506 Gross Point Road
Evanston, Illinois 60201

National Safety Council
444 North Michigan Avenue
Chicago, Illinois 60601
 312/527-4800

National Self-Help Clearinghouse
Graduate School & University Center
City University of New York
33 West 42nd Street, Room 1222
New York, New York 10036
 212/804-1259

RID
Remove Intoxicated Drivers
P.O. Box 520
Schenectady, New York 12301
 518/372-0034

RSA
Research Society on Alcoholism
c/o Boris Tabakoff, Ph.D., President
University of Illinois Medical Center
P.O. Box 6998
Chicago, Illinois 60680
 312/996-7606

Rutgers University
Center of Alcohol Studies Library
New Brunswick, New Jersey 08903
 201/932-4442

SADD
Students Against Drunk Driving
66 Diana Drive
Marlboro, Massachusetts 01752
 617/481-3588

The Christopher D. Smithers Foundation
P.O. Box 67
Mill Neck, New York 11765
 516/676-0067

DOT
U.S. Department of Transportation
National Highway Traffic Safety Administration
Office of Traffic Safety Programs
NTS-19
400 Seventh Street, S.W., Room 5130
Washington, D.C. 20590
 201/426-0874